Digging Into Skinwalker Ranch

Ryan T. Skinner

Cheryl Lynn Carter

Ryan Skinner and Cheryl Carter

Special thanks to: Ashley VanTassell, Christopher Bartel, Tyson Skinner, Whitney Skinner, and Melissa Peterson-Last

www.skinwalkerranch.org

www.chrisbartel.com

Twitter @SkinwalkerRyan

FB www.facebook.com/groups/481151978650301

Digging Into Skinwalker Ranch ©

"Skinwalker® and **Skinwalker Ranch®** are registered trademarks and used under license agreement with Adamantium Real Estate, LLC"

Copyright © 2021 by Ryan T. Skinner

ISBN – 9798743380893

Cover photos © Collection of the University of Maryland Art Gallery/Christopher M. Bartel (Homestead Three, 2010)

All rights reserved. No part of this book may be reproduced or transmitted in any form whatsoever without prior written permission from the author.

Foreword

By Thomas Winterton
Skinwalker Ranch Superintendent

In early 2016, the world famous Skinwalker Ranch exchanged hands. Robert Bigelow had sold the ranch to Brandon Fugal. Within weeks of purchasing the ranch, Ranch Manager Jim Morse had asked me to assist with inspecting and improving the facilities on the ranch.

In a short amount of time, my assistance had involved into a position within the ranch team, Ranch Superintendent. This position gave me access to all information the team had gathered pertaining to the ranch, which to my surprise, was very little. Bigelow had not offered up much in the way of information or evidence.

As a team, we were basically starting with a blank slate. This left us reaching out to individuals who had been involved during those almost 20 years. Much of the information gathered during the Bigelow days is under lock and key, with those involved tight lipped due to the Non-Disclosure Agreements they had signed with Mr. Bigelow.

Ryan Skinner and Cheryl Carter

I personally knew of stories that had allegedly happened on the ranch, but I had almost no knowledge of the individuals who had been associated with the ranch during the Bigelow years. One name that was brought to my attention in the beginning was that of an individual who had earned the title of "Public Enemy #1 from the Bigelow team. His name was Ryan Skinner. As the only local team member brought on by Brandon, I was asked to familiarize myself with who Ryan was. He had a history of sneaking onto the ranch. I also learned he had befriended a few individuals who worked for Mr. Bigelow and had obtained many documents and stories from these people.

I went to his website, www.SkinwalkerRanch.com and was surprised by the amount of data he had collected and organized. He had regularly trespassed onto the ranch and even alleged to have had experiences on the ranch. I realized it was just a matter of time before our paths would cross, and I secretly hoped that it would be me that caught him in the act of sneaking onto the ranch. I looked forward to making him an example to anyone who might entertain ideas of breaking onto the ranch. I had a terribly negative opinion of Ryan.

I was taken aback when Ryan unexpectedly reached out and asked permission to come on the ranch. I agreed to visit with him, and I was pleasantly surprised to find that he was not only respectful of the ranch and our team, but also very knowledgeable about the ranch during the Bigelow era.

Ryan has shared valuable insights and information with our team and had helped bridge the gap between the Bigelow era and the Adamantium era. I have been impressed by Ryan's desire to chase every lead and track down every clue. He has accumulated a library of knowledge in regards to Skinwalker Ranch much of it stemming with his ability to interview with past experiencers and witnesses, some of which have stopped publicly speaking about the ranch. Ryan has a wealth of knowledge when it comes to the history of Skinwalker Ranch.

Introduction

Ryan Skinner and Cheryl Carter

There are places in this world that have attributes far exceeding anything the mind could ever comprehend. According to some, this land holds on to secrets; secrets that whisper of mystical energies. The ancients spoke of the special powers of these anomalous places; places that hint to the possibility of stepping through portals enabling one to traverse time and move through other dimensions.

Such a place is located within the Uintah Basin that exudes a plethora of engaging energy. There is something so remarkable about the land that you will feel a special connection as it instantly touches your heart. And once it touches your soul, you will never be the same.

As you begin to delve deeper into the clandestineness of the land, you will find that you have crossed some sort of invisible line that is a point of no return. Before you realize, you will become one with it and the course of your life will be changed forever. It leaves you speechless, and yet turns you into a story teller because when you leave, you carry a part of it wherever you go.

This place is endowed with knowledge from many cultures that is intrinsically tied to the Earth; knowledge it might be willing to only share with a few. How many had come to this place in pursuit of a dream only to have realized something else? And yet, there are those who will always continue ... **Digging into Skinwalker Ranch.**

Digging Into

Skinwalker Ranch

Chapter 1 – The Path of the Skinwalker 9

Chapter 2 – Former Ranch Owners.......................14

Chapter 3 – Christopher Bartel 50

Chapter 4 – Guard Reports 57

Chapter 5 – Incident Reports 88

Chapter 6 – That One Time 93

Chapter 7 – Kryder Exploration 106

Chapter 8 – Bill Muldoon 112

Chapter 9 – Somewhere In the Skies 118

Chapter 10 – Utah UFO Statistics....................... 125

Chapter 11 – Utah UFOs
  MUFON Witness Sightings.............….. 130

Chapter 12 – Utah UFOs
  NURFORC Witness Sightings ….. 143

Chapter 13 – Crop Circles… 148

Chapter 14 – Cattle Mutilations 158

Chapter 15 – Hitchhikers ….......................... 184

Chapter 16 - Remote-Viewing of the Ranch 201

Chapter 17 – Implants 215

Chapter 18 – No Trespassing 219

Chapter 19 – With the Shadows of the Ridge 225

Chapter 20 – Beyond the Continuum 232

Chapter 1

The Path of the Skinwalker

The Skinwalker is a shape-shifter who according to Navajo legend has the ability to assume at will the form of an animal usually a wolf. They are also known by the name "yee naaldlooshii" meaning "with it, he goes on all fours."

The Navajo believe there are places on Earth where the powers of both good and evil are present. Those powers can be harnessed for either. Medicine men that are taught to be the bridge between the Earth people and the spirit world use these powers to heal while those who would choose to practice witchcraft seek to direct the spiritual powers to cause harm.

Navajo witchcraft is known as the "Witchery Way." The highest level is known as "clizyati" meaning "pure evil." In order to achieve this level, one must kill a close blood relative. Witchery Way uses the bones from human corpses to make tools and corpse dust that are used to curse, harm, or kill intended victims. Corpse dust is made from ground cadaver bones, partially the fingertips and the back of the skull. The dust is blown into the face of the intended victim. Once inhaled, it incapacitates the victim putting them a zombie-like state. The Skinwalker can then control them by way of telepathic suggestions.

Skinwalkers are described as being not quite human and not quite animal and are able to control the creatures of the night. They possess supernatural powers enabling them to run faster than any vehicle and to be able to jump high cliffs. They are able to read a person's mind, control their thoughts and behavior, and cause illness or death. Their eyes are not human-like. Making eye contact with one will prove deadly as they absorb the person's life force giving themselves more.

Many times they can be seen running through the night, sometimes turning into a fiery ball, leaving streaks of color light behind them. More times they appear in front of vehicles hoping to cause an accident. There are times they are tricksters making sounds around homes such as knocking on windows and banging on doors.

Digging Into Skinwalker Ranch

On October 31, 1862, the United States army, in order to gain control of the land for mining purposes, made war on the Navajo using a scorched-earth method to destroy their fields, houses, and livestock. However, even before they were defeated, Congress was authorizing the establishment of a reservation at Fort Sumner near Bosque Redonda along the Pecos River in New Mexico. Some officers disagreed with this decision because of its contaminated water and minimal provisions of fire wood. Nonetheless, the reservation was established.

The fighting continued and during a final standoff in January of 1864 at Canyon de Chelly, the Navajo surrendered to Kit Carson and his troops. In 1864, the Navajo were expelled from their land by the government and forced to walk to the Bosque Redondo reservation consisting of forty square miles that was near the Fort Sumner post. The 3,000 tribal members walked 300 miles along what became known as the Long Walk of the Navajo.

The Navajo called the reservation "Hweeldi" meaning "land of suffering." During those years many of the tribe's people turned to shape-shifting in order to escape the terrible living conditions and the government's attempt at cultural assimilation. Upon realizing they had made a mistake, the government entered into the Treaty of 1868 with the Navajo, where they were allowed to return to their homeland in the Four Corners area. The shape-shifters were still among them.

One day, some tribal members found a collection of witch items wrapped in a copy of the Treaty of 1868. Fearing the witches were going to bring bad times upon them again, they sought them out. In 1878, 40 Navajo suspected witches were killed during the Navajo Witch Purge in order to restore balance to the tribe.

In Utah, there's a place located near the Ute Reservation where the tribe always thought the Navajo had put a curse on the land in retribution for some perceived transgressions. The Ute refer to this place as the Path of the Skinwalker and display animal skulls on the fence posts warning the Skinwalkers to stay away from their property.

© Christopher M. Bartel

These 512 acres located along the southern border of the Uintah-Ouray Reservation east of the Duchesne-Uintah County border are known as ...

Skinwalker Ranch

Chapter 2

Previous Owners Of Skinwalker Ranch

Allotment and Homesteading

<u>Allotment</u>

On February 8, 1887, the Dawes Act regulating land rights on tribal lands was introduced by Republican Senator Henry L. Dawes of Massachusetts. The act stated that all Indians on or off the reservation would be allotted a tract of land, from 20 up to 160 acres. The Indian Appropriations Act of May 27, 1902, required all allotments within the reservation to be completed by September 1, 1905 and any surplus to be opened to the public domain.

By June 1905, all allotments were granted for those living on the Uintah-Ouray Reservation. The remaining land was opened up for Homesteading.

Ute delegation of 1905 for the final negotiations on opening the Uintah and Ouray Reservation. Front: Appah, Arrive; center: Red Cap, David Copperfield, Charlie Shavanaux, Wee-che; rear: Wallace Stark, Charley Mack, John Duncan, Suckive, unknown, Boco White, unknown. Courtesy Smithsonian Institution.

1905 Final Negotiations on opening the Uintah-Ouray Reservation named after Chief Ouray. (Note: Charlie Shavanaux, father of Monk Shavanaux the first owner of the Skinwalker Ranch property)

Homesteading

In 1869, the federal government opened a Land Office in Salt Lake City. There had already been laws in place to govern the process of acquiring land. One such law enacted on April 24, 1820, was the "Act Making Provision for the Sale of Public Land". This law stated that surveyed land would be offered at a two week public sale. The land would be sold in quarter sections which were three miles square and sold to the highest bidder. All payments of not less than $1.25 per acre were due on that day.

The Homestead Act of 1862 provided free grants of public land to any person who was a citizen, over 21, or head of a household. These homesteaders were allowed to claim 160 acres. In order to obtain a "Patent," they would be required to improve and cultivate the land, erect a fence, and maintain residency for at least five years.

Digging Into Skinwalker Ranch

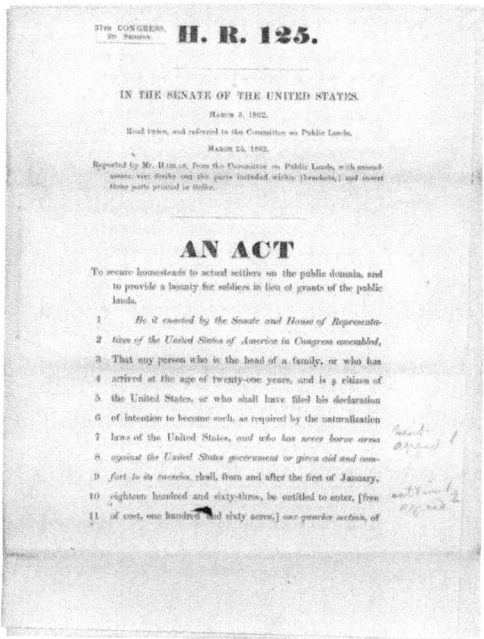

Homestead Act of 1862

July 14, 1905, President Theodore Roosevelt declared all unallotted lands in the Uintah Indian Reservation to be open for settlement under the provisions of the Homestead Act. Of the original 2,080,000 acre Uintah Reservation, an estimated 104,000 acres were allotted to individual Indian families and 1,072,000 were allotted in trust for their benefit. The remaining 1,004,000 acres were returned to Public Domain.

Ryan Skinner and Cheryl Carter

Monk Shavanaugh/Shavanaux
July 7, 1905- 1916

Monk "Ne-Goots" Shavanaugh/Shavanaux, of the Uncompahgre Ute Nation, was born in 1868 on the Uintah-Ouray Reservation, Utah. He was the oldest of thirteen children to Charley and Ta-a-he Shavanaugh who were originally from the Colorado Ute Reservation. They were the southern Utes known as White River Utes. After a treaty was signed in 1861, they relocated to the Uintah-Ouray Reservation in Utah.

He married Koeweats "Hoo-ule-ats" Macheveant who was born in 1882 on the White Rocks Reservation, Utah. They had a son Charley from Koeweats previous marriage. He held a position with the Indian Tribal Police.

They had a son Charley from Koeweats previous marriage. He held a position with the Indian Tribal Police.

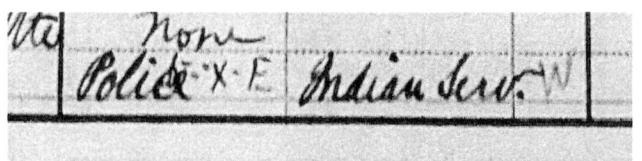

Tribal Police

Digging Into Skinwalker Ranch

120	Chee-voo-rah	Shavanaugh Julia	F	Daughter	16
121	Che-gu-cat	Shavanaugh Mary	F	Grand-daughter	14
122	Monk Shavanaugh	Shavanaugh Monk	M	Father	37
123	Koo-we-ats	Shavanaugh Koeweats	F	Wife	23
124		Shavanaugh Charley	M	Stepson	7
125	Nanna-ka-poos	Nannakapoos	F	Wife	46
6	Henry Jim	Jim Henry	M	Father	61

Indian Census 1905

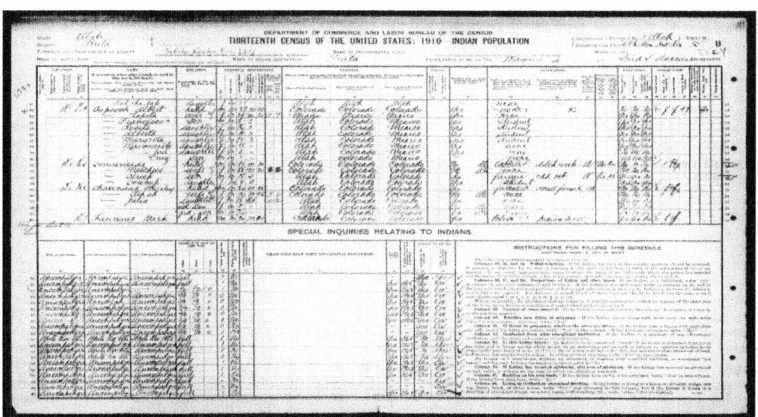

Indian Census 1910

19

On July 7, 1905, he was allotted 328.72 acres within Section 5 and 33 by way of the Ballard Indian Fee Patent. The ownership and use of this patent is overseen by the Bureau of Land Management's Vernal Field Office. This Indian Fee Patent falls under U.S. Code Title 254 Indians, Statute 014, Page 703: Providing Patent of Allotment for Ute Indians-Uintah and Ouray Reservation.

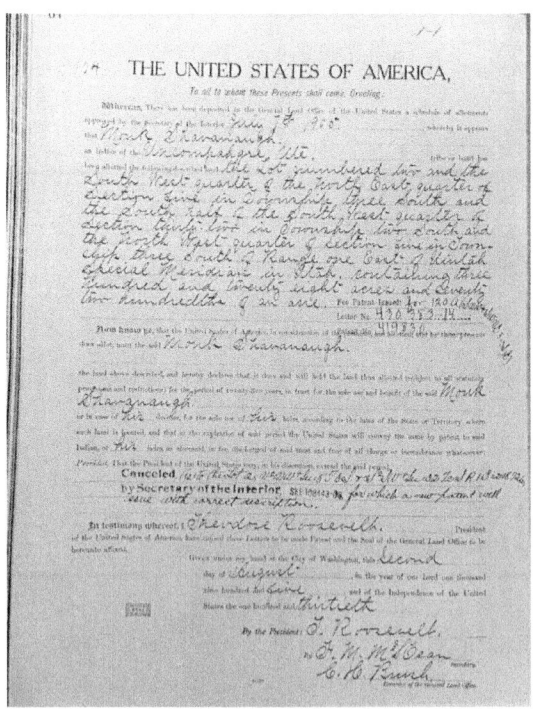

Allotment July 7, 1905

Amendment to Deed August 15, 1916

Ryan Skinner and Cheryl Carter

Henry Ralph Litster

June 11, 1930-1945

Henry Ralph Litster, the son of John Campbell Litster was born August 8, 1892, in Vernal, Utah. He and his twin sister Henriette were the youngest of four children.

John Campbell Litster was born in Cobinbeth, Scotland, in 1870 and came to America with his family when he was eleven years old.

Henry worked alongside his father on his horse ranch.

He was drafted into the Army during WWI on June 6, 1918 and served as Private in Company G, 157 Infantry until March 28, 1919. Upon returning home, he married Ferris Omega Hall on October 16, 1919. They had no children. They eventually moved from the family ranch to Ft. Duchesne.

Ferris passed away in 1929 and he later married Ruth Miller Behun of Rock Springs, Wyoming on March 15, 1952. They had a son named Quentin Ralph and a step-son Paul Behun.

Over the course of his lifetime, he worked a mine, worked with the Indian Agency at the government saw mill where he was a ranger, assisted with building several Indian schoolhouses in White Rocks, and owned a cattle ranch in the Basin.

Henry Litster

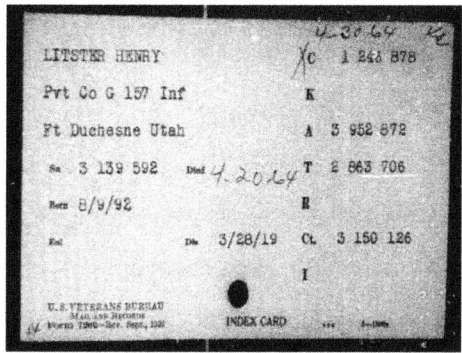

WWI Army ID

WWI Army Discharge

1940 Census shows he worked in a mine

On May 25, 1945, Henry Litster petitioned to transfer irrigation rights from one part of his property to another.

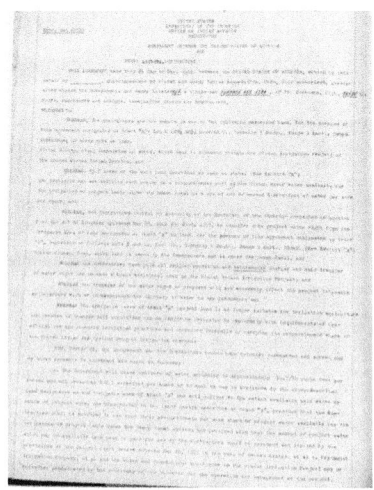

Petition to transfer Irrigation Rights

> M 80 acres—$100 42
> Henry Litster Lt Duchesne Utah—Lots 3 4 Sec 15 Twp 2 S R 1 E, USM Less 1 06 acres in F A P 94 D 55 62 acres—$12 82

Delioquent Taxeson Land, 1943 Vernal Express

> Henry Litster, c-o Ruth M. Litster, P.O. Box 18, Roosevelt, Utah—Lots 3 and 4; Sec. 15, T2S, R1E, USM, Less 1.06 acres in FA project, 55.62 acres—$80.09.

Delinquent Taxes on Land, 1944 Vernal Express

> —$12 92
> JOHN LITSTER Per Henry Litster Fort Duchesne Utah Lots 3 & 4 of Sec 15 Twp 2 S R 1E USM—56 68 acres —$19 30
> UNION CENTRAL LIFE INS CO

John Lister Assumed Delinquent Taxes
1950 Vernal Express, February 4, 1913

Continued delinquent taxes played a key role in his decision to sell the property.

25

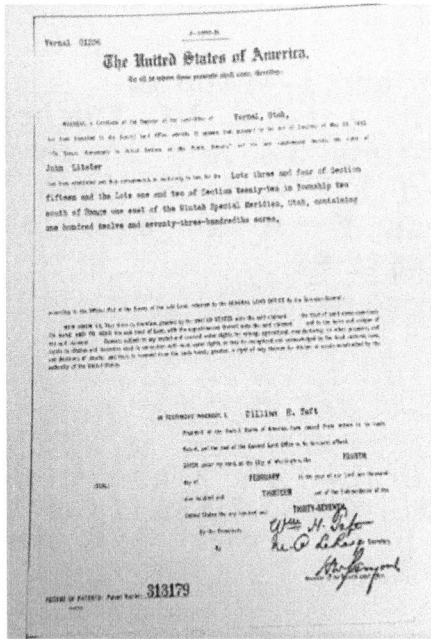

John Lister
Homestead Entry Patent Number 313179

On February 4, 1913, Henry Litster's father John Campbell Litster was issued a land patent through the Uintah and Ouray Reservation Homestead Patent. Ownership and use of this patent is overseen by the Bureau of Land Management's Vernal Field Office. This Homestead Entry Original Patent falls under U.S. Code Title 43 Public Lands; Section 161; Statute 012; Page 0392. An Act to Secure Homesteads to Actual Settlers on the Public Domain. Upon his father's death October 12, 1942, Henry became the heir to his land.

Sale of the land to Benton McMullin Locke on June 11, 1945: Lot 2, Section 5, Township 3 South of Range 1 east of the Uintah Special Meridian containing forty acres without water rights.

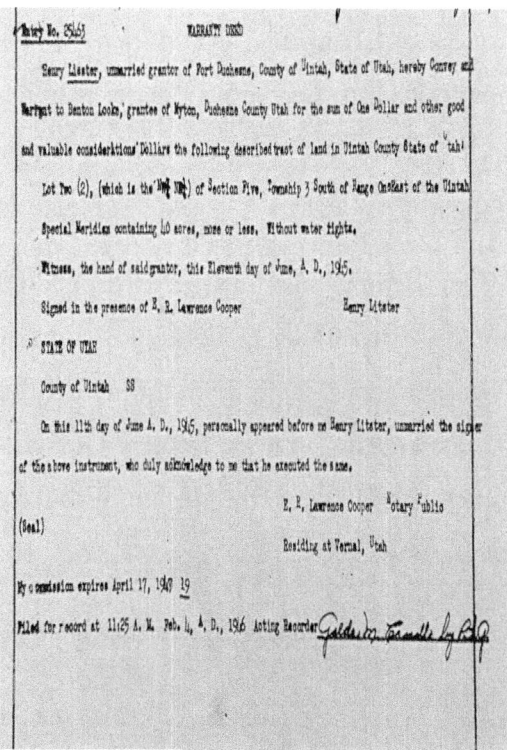

Warranty Deed Number 25463

Ryan Skinner and Cheryl Carter

Benton McMullin & Ona Ora Locke
1928-1934

Benton McMullin Locke, the second oldest of six children to William Columbus Locke and Leatha Florence Lee was born on June 17, 1899, in White Plains, Kentucky. He worked alongside his father on the family farm and dreamed of one day having his own. When he was 28, he moved to Uintah, Utah to pursue his dream. It was here that he met Ona Ora Bryant and they married on September 23, 1929, in Uintah, Utah.

Ona Ora Bryant, the third of six children to Ira Samuel Bryant and Esther Ella Douglas, was born on March 18, 1910, in Independence, Utah. During their marriage, they had five children, Mullan Douglas, Benetta Gossett, William Ira, and including two children who died at birth John Joseph and Arthur Douglas.

Benton McMullin Locke

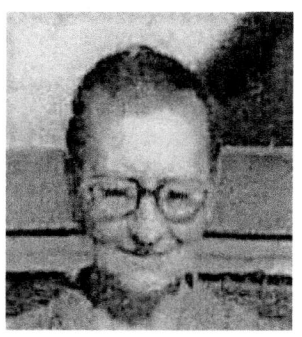
Ona Ora Locke

Courtesy of the Locke Family
Benton center back wearing dark overalls.

Benton and Ona on the right

```
U.S.M. 45.21 acres—$51.70.
    Benton Locke, Myton, Utah—
Lot 1 Sec. 5 Twp. 3 S, R. 1 E.,
U.S.M, 42 68 acres—$79.27.
    Benton Locke, Myton, Utah—
SE¼ NE¼ Sec. 5 Twp. 3 S.,
R. 1 E., U S.M., 40 acres—$4 53.
    Benton Locke, Myton, Utah—
NW ¼ NE¼, (Lot 2) Sec. 5 Twp.
3 S, R 1 E., U S M., 42.79 acres
    $33 87.
```

Delinquent taxes for ten consecutive years
played a key role in his decision to sell the property

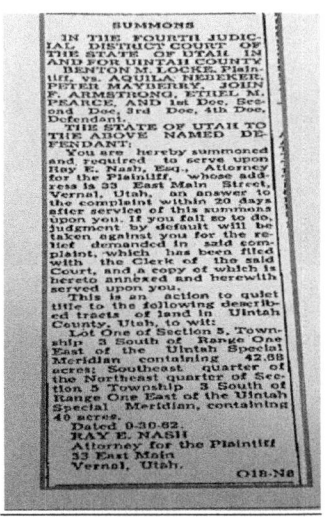

Action for a Quiet Title June 28, 1962

78B-6-1301 Quiet Title in Utah: Grounds to settle tax issues with a property.

Action on: Lot 1 Sec 5 Twp 3 S, R 1 E, USM. 42.68 acres and SE ¼ NE ¼ Sec 5 Twp 3 S, R 1 E, USM, 40 acres.

Sale of the land to Kenneth Myers and Edith Myers on April 14, 1961, for the sum of $5,000: Lot 1, Section 5, Township 3 South, Range 1 East, Uintah Special Meridian, containing 42.68 acres … Lot 2 (NW ¼ NE ¼) of Section 5, Township 3 South, Range 1 East, Uintah Special Meridian, containing 42.79 acres … the southwest quarter of the Northeast quarter of Section 5, Township 3 South, Range 1 East, Uintah Special Meridian, containing 40 acres … together with all water rights and water appurtenant, including 36 shares of Indian Irrigation water rights …reserving ½ interest of all oil, gas, and mineral rights in, on, or under said land.

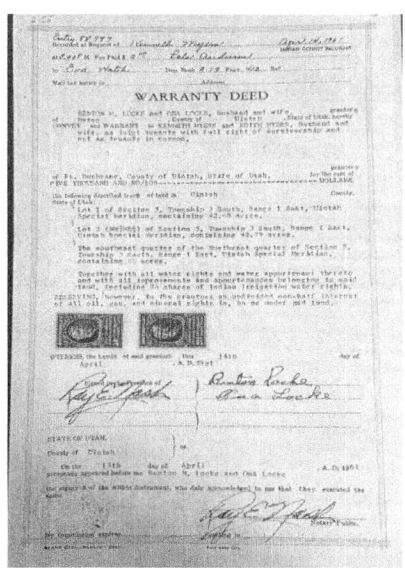

Ryan Skinner and Cheryl Carter

Kenneth and Edith Myers
1934-1994

Edith Child, the youngest of six children to George Newport Child and Florence Willes Child, was born on November 8, 1905 in Lehi, Utah. Her mother Florence experienced cardiac complications during a premature birth, which resulted in her passing away when Edith was only two weeks old. She was raised by her mother's sister Achsah Schow until when at age 16 she moved to Salt Lake City to live with her father and family.

She attended the University of Utah where she was a member of the debate team. After graduating, she became a teacher in Salt Lake City. On April 17, 1927, she married Kenneth John Myers at the Latter Day Saints temple in Salt Lake City.

Kenneth John Meyers, the oldest of four children to John Whiting Myers and Emma Elizabeth Garner Myers, was born on November 5, 1903 in American Fork, Utah. He attended Brigham Young University. In 1923 at the age of nineteen, he was ordained to the office of Elder. Each Elder is part of an organized group of priesthood holders known as an Elders Quorum. He received the rank of Elder 3rd

Quorum and served as a missionary as part of the British Mission from 1923-1925. Upon returning home, he worked as a telephone operator for American Express for seven years.

As fate would have it, he met Edith and they married. The following year as they were awaiting an addition to their family, Baby Boy Meyers unfortunately was premature at seven months resulting in him being stillborn on April 11, 1928. They had no more children during their marriage.

Kenneth always had a dream; a dream of owning a ranch. In 1933, he and Edith left the city behind as he pursued his adventure. They went to the Uintah Basin and talked with the Indian Agency. It was there, that they were able to lease some land from Benton Locke. On April 14, 1961, he sold the property to them through a Warranty Deed.

Edith relates their story calling it "The Saga: How to become a Rancher."

"First, you marry a man who has a dream of having a ranch and making it come true. Kenneth's Uncle Albert, brother of Emma Myers, had a sheep ranch and Kenneth worked for him a lot. To him it was" Paradise". The depression came and jobs were scarce. We decided it was now or never! Kenneth made a trailer from an old car frame. We loaded it with a bed, table, two chairs, machinery donated by his dad and Grandpa Gardner. We set out for the Uintah Basin. At the Indian Agency, they sent us to a place to lease, not far from Fort Duchesne. It had a three-room house, but it had been used as a "horse shade". We found the windows from the horse owner, scrubbed out the manure, whitewashed the two front rooms, and moved in after ten days of living in the yard and sleeping in the car. It was a drought that summer, no water for crops. They cut tumbleweeds and stacked them like hay to feed the cattle next winter. Irrigation water: you filled two 50 gallon barrels when any came down the canal. Drinking water: we hauled in a ten gallon can from Fort Duchesne. We bought a team of horses: Doll and Bird. One was balky and the other got the bellyache. A neighbor boy had a riding horse he wanted to sell, but we didn't have any more '"horse money". They finally made a deal, a pair of used cowboy boots and an old sombrero, and the horse was all ours. He was a bucking horse in rodeos, and he could unload you in a hurry! His name was "Dine", short for "Dynamite," but he was a real cow pony. There was a place about a mile farther up the road, a real ranch with a four room log house and crops. It was for sale. We moved that fall and it was "paradise!" That was the beginning of being a real rancher in 1934, and it still is, 60 years later."

Kenneth and Edith Myers on the Ranch

Kenneth Myers passed away on April 26, 1987 and Edith was issued an Affidavit of Surviving Joint Tenant. The document states: "Edith Myers, being first duly sworn, deposes and says: That she is the surviving wife of Kenneth Myers, who died on the 26th day of April, 1987, at Roosevelt, Duchesne County, State of Utah, and was a resident of Uintah County, State of Utah, at the time of his death; that said Kenneth Myers was one of the joint tenant grantees named in that certain Warranty Deed dated April 14, 1961, and recorded April 14, 1961, in Book A-79, page 412, wherein the following described property was deeded to Kenneth Myers and Edith Myers, husband and wife, as joint tenants with full right of survivorship and not as tenants in common, said land being situated in Uintah County, State of Utah, to wit …

…That the joint tenancy in the above described tract of land terminated upon the death of said Kenneth Myers as shown on the certified copy of the Utah Certificate of Death, No. 143-87002351 which is attached hereto and by this reference made a part hereof and by virtue of such termination, title to said property is vested in the surviving joint tenant, Edith Myers."

Edith Myers continued to live on the ranch until she passed away on March 3, 1994. At that time, Kenneth's brother Garth Myers was appointed Personal Representative of the estate.

Kenneth and Edith Myers

Baby Boy Myers

The document states as follows:

"In the Eighth Judicial District Court of Uintah County, State of Utah in the matter of the Estate of Edith Child Myers deceased. Garth G. Myers was duly appointed and qualified as Personal Representative of the estate of the above named Decedent on the 19th day of April, 1994, by the Court with all authority thereto.

Administration of the estate is unsupervised. These letters are issued to evidence the appointment, qualification, and authority of said Personal Representative."

Dr. Garth G. Myers

The Myers estate was divided equally among the four surviving siblings. On August 8, 1994, the property was sold

Ryan Skinner and Cheryl Carter

to Terry Nolan Sherman and Gwen Ann Sherman. The Warranty Deed states as follows:

"Garth G. Myers, as duly appointed and qualified personal representative of the Estate of Edith Childs Myers, AKA Edith Myers, in the matter of Probate No. 943800015-ES in the Eighth Judicial District Court of Uintah County, State of Utah, grantor of the Salt Lake City, County of Salt Lake City, County of Salt Lake, State of Utah, hereby convey and warrant to:

Terry N. Sherman and Gwen A. Sherman, husband and wife, as joint tenants with full rights of survivorship …"

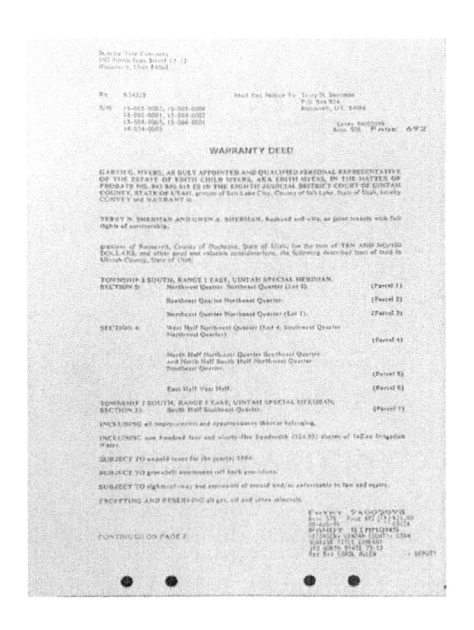

Warranty Deed Number 94005098

Digging Into Skinwalker Ranch

Terry and Gwen Sherman
1994-1996

Terry Nolan Sherman the son of Addison LaMar Sherman and Caroline Price was born in Pomerence, Arizona. He was one of six children. They moved to Utah when he was seventeen.

He married Gwen Ann Sherman daughter of Robert and Ann Oldson who was born in Utah. Terry worked and raised cattle on leased land while Gwen worked at a bank.

In 1994, they purchased property from the Myers Estate in hopes of fulfilling a dream, however it soon proved to be something else. Almost from the beginning they found themselves surrounded by a plethora of high strangeness: strange lights and orbs, sounds, disembodied voices, and ghostly figures.

Thinking things couldn't possibly get more unsettling, the strange phenomena proceeded to escalate as they began to observe what appeared to be portals opening and closing in the sky accompanied by unidentified flying objects.

The Shermans said they witnessed three types of UFOs over the duration of their time living there: small box-shaped crafts approximately eight feet long, forty foot long craft, and a ship approximately the size of several football fields.

Gwen's Story

as told to Ryan Skinner: "The Ranch was a dream we had for our family to raise cattle and have a family business. But it became a broken dream. The Ranch has grown into something I would have never believed. When we found the Ranch, we thought that we had found Heaven, but it turned out to be Hell."

"When Garth Myers the executor of the estate of Ken and Edith Myers sold us the Ranch, he never mentioned anything to us about what was going on there. All he did was instruct us not to dig with a backhoe or move the big rock by the middle Homestead that appeared to have rolled off the hill."

"One day, we were chasing some cows that got out and came across a mutilated cow pile hidden in the sagebrush. You know how to tell the difference between a natural death and a mutilated cow. Predators will not touch the mutilated cow. With the natural cause of death of a cow, coyotes, crows, and buzzards will eat it and then drag off the bones. A mutilated cow stays intact for months until the dried hide starts to fall apart. They had about 30 in the secret pile."

"When Garth Myers would stop by to talk, he would ask if we had anything weird happen. He said nothing ever happened and yet he always asked the weirdest questions. When he was asked about the mutilated cows and if his brother had any, he just got back into his truck muttering."

"Mrs. Betts, a neighbor, told my husband she would see strange balls of light. The first time she saw one was when she was six or seven and it bounced across the field. She also saw crafts in the sky. The activity is on a ten year cycle. Every ten years the craft was different. She was told as a young girl to never go outside after dark when activity was high."

"When there were two of us, Terry and I started not looking at the same thing. One of us would look and observe the obvious and the other would search for something else. It was like something was trying to distract us."

"There are small caves. The kids found goat horns in a tunnel. It looked like it went on forever. They said it had an evil, dark feeling and never went back."

"Orbs ... There's a light blue swirling one about the size of a golf ball. The red orb is usually seen when chaos or something bad is happening. It chases the cattle through the fields and scares them. The white orb is usually attached to missing time. Your watch will stop and when you awaken, you will find yourself in a totally different place."

"At night time, sometimes a white hole will open up and shadow creatures will crawl out. You will hear voices in different languages from above. I've seen ships come through a portal and leave through one."

"We've seen wolves. I believe they live in another dimension and travel through at will. I've seen two Natives; one is old and the other is younger and runs with the wolves. When I saw him he looked as startled and spooked as I was. He was standing on the edge of the ridge top. There's a partial Medicine Wheel there. I always hear loud drumming and he appears."

Terry's Story: "My first eventful sighting on the Ranch was April, 15, 1994. One night, we were out in the field waiting for a calf to be born. Suddenly, we saw something like a small vehicle that looked like it had one headlight. We thought it might be the neighbor on his tractor looking for a lost cow. We walked down to within 100 yards of it and it proceeded to move away. There was no sound and it went quite a distance over wet ground."

"It would project a light out in front of it almost like a spotlight, but it was brighter like sunlight. It was about a 20-25 foot beam. Then it went across the top of several barbed wire fences. At first I thought they drove through the fences, but the fence was untouched."

"It went several yards ahead of us and at about 30 mph went over some trees that were 30-40 feet tall. Whatever it was, it was almost like a square, slightly smaller at the top than the bottom, 8 feet long, 6 feet wide, and 6 feet tall."

"After that night, we continued to see several strange crafts in the night sky; triangle, diamond, and boomerang shaped. Every time that happened, we would find a mutilation the next day. Usually this would happen on the darkest night of the month."

"Sometimes I would see these orbs of light. When this happened, I would have images run through my mind; images of people, people I didn't know … flashing quickly though my mind, one after another, talking to one another in a conversation I couldn't quite hear."

"One day, I had a dream of two men wearing some sort of uniform with some sort of insignia on their collar. They were talking, but I couldn't quite hear what they were saying. Suddenly, I found myself looking out the window of some craft and seeing the ground below me. A few minutes later I was back on the ground and watching this craft in the sky. I heard a voice in my head say, "It wouldn't do any good if we tried to explain to him because he would never understand what we are doing."

"Was that a terrible dream or did it actually happen? All I know is I will never be able to get that experience out of my mind. That's when we decided it was time to move."

"After countless interviews and failed attempts to connect with someone who might assist them in determining exactly what was occurring on their property, the totality of the strangeness began to take its toll on them both psychologically and financially. So only eighteen months later they decided to sell."

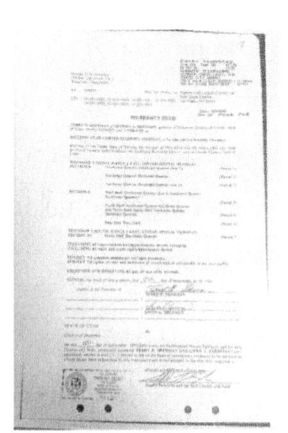

Warranty Deed Number 96005042
September 5, 1996

Digging Into Skinwalker Ranch

Terry Sherman on the Ranch

Gwen Sherman

Ryan Skinner and Cheryl Carter

Robert Bigelow

1996-2016

Robert Thomas Bigelow was born May 12, 1945, in Las Vegas, Nevada. On February 4, 2004, he married Diane Mary Mona. She was the daughter of Michael Mona and Bertha Elizabeth Eckel born April 9, 1947 in Camden, New Jersey and later moved to Las Vegas, Nevada. They have two sons.

Robert Thomas Bigelow   Diane Mary Mona Bigelow

He graduated from Arizona State University where he studied banking and real estate. During the late 1960's through the 1990's he developed commercial real estate hotels. He owns the hotel chain Budget Suites of America.

Digging Into Skinwalker Ranch

Robert Bigelow on the Ranch

BAASS ID

In 1995, he founded the National Institute of Discovery Science, NIDS, in order to advance the research and study of numerous paranormal areas, including Ufology and cattle mutilation. He had always wondered if we were alone in the universe and what happens to us when we die. Robert's interest in Near Death Experiences and Consciousness was most likely derived from the passing of his son.

After hearing about the high strangeness of a particular property in Utah, in 1996, he purchased this property for $250,000 from Terry and Gwen Sherman who had only owned it for two years. Here he would carry out his research hoping to find answers.

In 1999, he founded Bigelow Aerospace Advanced Space Studies (BAASS). Around 2009, BAASS entered into a working agreement with the Mutual UFO Network (MUFON). He was of the theory that there was an opening or tear in the electromagnetic fabric of our planet located on or around the property.

After conducting copious amounts of secret investigating on the property, on April 1, 2016, Robert Bigelow sold the property to Adamantium Holdings, a Utah based company.

Digging Into Skinwalker Ranch

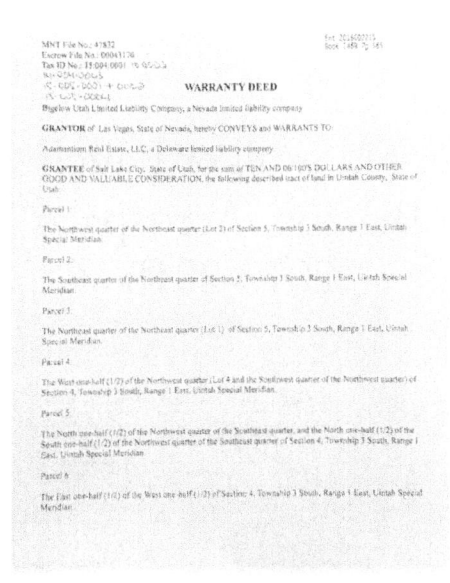

Warranty Deed April 1, 2016
Sale of the Ranch to Adamantium Holdings

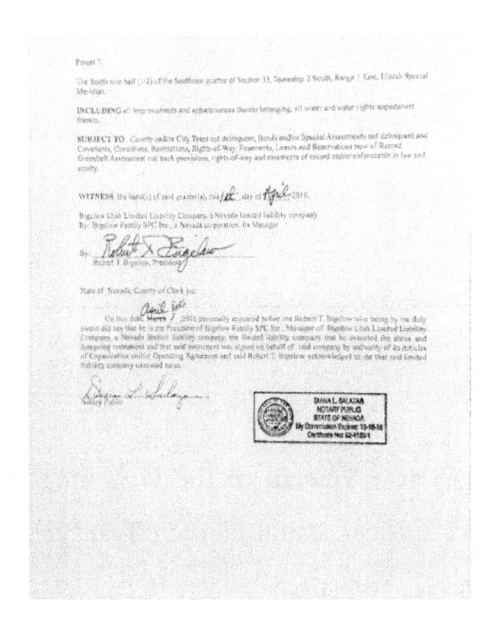

Chapter 3
Christopher M. Bartel
Former Skinwalker Ranch Guard Bigelow Aerospace 2010-2018

© Christopher M. Bartel

Cheryl Carter: "Chris, can you tell me about your background?"

Chris Bartel: "I'm a Veteran of the U.S. Air Force, former Security Police Officer at the Nevada Test Site, and former Guard to Bigelow Aerospace."

Cheryl Carter: "How long were you employed at Bigelow Aerospace?"

Chris Bartel: "I was employed as a Security Guard from September 25, 2010, until March 2018."

Cheryl Carter: "What did the experience of being a guard entail?"

Chris Bartel: "We did a lot of work at night. That included walking the grounds and keeping our eyes open to whatever we might encounter. And you learn quickly that the place has secrets and anomalous things. My first experience was in 2010, when it had only been my second week on the property. Suddenly, we encountered a wolf, but it was not any ordinary wolf. This one was the size of a large deer. It was huge!"

Cheryl Carter: "What happened when you saw the wolf? Did it see you too?"

Chris Bartel: "It caught my attention that's for sure. It was just there and then it was gone. It was a very unique experience. That's when I started to carry my own personal camera around. To better document possible evidence but to also capture how gorgeous the property was.

Cheryl Carter: "Did you notice anything strange after this encounter?"

Chris Bartel: "Well, a short time later I noticed two strange lumps that felt like there was something inside; one on my knee and the other on my right forearm. I finally went to the VA and the doctor examined them. He also did an MRI, but it was inconclusive. He thought they were just cysts. I still have them, but they don't bother me. All I can say for sure is that what I saw was no ordinary wolf."

Cheryl Carter: "Could this be an implant you received after your close encounter at the Ranch?"

Chris Bartel: "It is the ranch so anything is possible, I hope it is not, which is why I'm still currently getting medical tested. Anyway, I carried on and by 2011 we were down to working solo with just the dogs. The first night it felt a little strange being all alone. There I was miles away from the rest of the world. What if something happened to me? But then I thought this wasn't any different than being out in the country like back home in Kansas."

Cheryl Carter: "What did you find as you and the dog worked the property each night?"

Chris Bartel: "After awhile I began to find arrowheads and other artifacts. I wasn't doing any digging. They would just be there in my path. It was so strange. Why was I finding these? What was the property trying to tell me? I almost felt as if I was being guided. All I knew was that it was important; so important that I made a spreadsheet noting each one, its color/size, and where they were found.

© Christopher M. Bartel

Thinking this was very important to the research being done, I took my findings to Bigelow Aerospace management. However instead of the managers being pleased, I was told that the arrowheads were of no significance to their study of the Ranch. Management seemed more concerned with looking up at the sky. I heard rumors about other guards being asked to stop digging before the Utes found out. They concluded with telling me to stop documenting the findings.

Cheryl Carter: "And did you?"

Chris Bartel: "How could I? And in all actuality they wouldn't let me. Somehow I knew this find was much bigger than any work being done there so I continued to record everything for myself. As time went by, I found more arrowheads and artifacts. I noticed they were in specific locations and there appeared to be a pattern. It had to mean something."

Cheryl Carter: "Maybe they were trying to tell you their story. The reason they did that was possibly because they knew you have Native blood. They connected with you and trusted you."

Chris Bartel: "I believe that too. The Native ground retains its energy. I found so many arrowheads, axe heads, and other artifacts that this had to be where somebody made their home. There were a lot by the East Gate, the second dog run, and the Mesa side. I actually took one unique arrowhead to an expert. He told me it was very old and most likely Freemont from 1100 A.D. making it a thousand years old! I also found evidence of what appeared to be the place where they held Lodge and sweats. One time when I was by Homestead 3, I heard the sound of drums."

Cheryl Carter: "That is amazing and coincides with what I "saw" when I remote-viewed there. I saw a man, a protector, building a sacred fire and entering into a Lodge."

Chris Bartel: "Yes, a Lodge. I found what appeared to be several Grandfathers all in one spot. I do remember another guard telling me he saw a native man wearing traditional ancient attire walking the ridgeline. According to this guard, incredible as it sounds, this stranger transformed into a wolf before his eyes!"

Cheryl Carter: "I saw him standing at the edge of a small stream near a beaver dam."

Chris Bartel: "Yes, there is a stream that runs through the property. There's a beaver dam with two beavers. It's possible that he protects the land too maybe because of the past.

I've tried several times to go back to the southern tree line area. However, every time it's as if something subconsciously warns me to stay away. And speaking of warnings, there's a very strange sight on the adjacent property to the west. That property actually belongs to the Utes. Most people don't know this land is bordered by Native land.

When you look beyond the fence, you will see animal skins tied to the fence posts. My mother who grew up on several Indian reservations told me that was a warning to keep bad energy away."

Cheryl Carter: "Do you ever wish you could go back there?"

Chris Bartel: "Yes, in a heartbeat! I feel that my spirit is soul bound to the property"

© Christopher M. Bartel

Chapter 4

Guard Reports

The following are actual Guard Reports from Skinwalker Ranch from 2009-

Utah Ranch

Daily Ranch Summary 04/18/09
Submitted by S/O Johnny

Information

- From 8:10 p.m. till 8:37 p.m. Jean and I took and reviewed pictures.
- In picture #P4180035, at 8:13 p.m. I had a very bright blue/white round object. The picture was taken facing northeast approximately 15 yards from the single wide trailer. The object looked to be just in front of the trees about then height of the trailer roof. The part that makes this so unusual is that it was still

light outside, and yet this object appeared very bright and clear.

- No one came to the gate during the night.

Utah Ranch

Daily Ranch Summary 05/02/09
Submitted by: S/O Anthony

Information

- I reviewed and burned the video with Jean. In the video from 4/27/09, there is a strange light in the sky that is noteworthy. I have elaborated on it below.
- No one came to the gate during the night.
- I cannot patrol the west side due to rain making the road muddy.
- Nothing outstanding happened during the night.

Conclusion: The light appears at approximately 2104:52 in the upper right portion of the video, just above the ridge. The light goes behind the ridge then reappears toward the middle of the screen. The light then turns toward us and we can hear what sounds to be an engine. The engine sound is heard between approximately 2106:12 and 2106:41. The light turns back toward the ridge and disappears at approximately 2106:55. It may just be an airplane, but the light seems to be awfully bright compared to the other airplanes that we have seen. Jean and I did not see this event in person.

Utah Ranch

Daily Summary 06/30/09
Submitted by S/OC

Information

On this day I, S/OC conducted normal security operations with no incidents to report. Mr. Bigelow and three guests arrived on the property today. In the evening, Jean and I took and reviewed photographs and there is nothing unusual to report.

Ryan Skinner and Cheryl Carter

Utah Ranch

Daily Report 08/21/2009
Submitted by: Thomas

Daily Summary Events:

1. Verbal threat over the radio
2. East Gate
3. Run 2
4. Homestead 2
5. Homestead 3
6. Investigating Notes

1 – Verbal threat over the radio

Homestead 1, Mark and I received a verbal threat over the radio. "I don't know if you can hear me, but I'm killing you!" followed by a lot of garbled nonsense. At the time, I was reading Dr. Colm's book, "Hunt for the Skinwalker." It should be noted that the threat was coming from the same channel as last night's transmission, channel 21.

2 – East Gate

Quiet night at the East Gate although we did hear what might have been gunshot. Subsequent scans of the area using NVGs (Night Vision Goggles) turned up to nothing. Took some pictures when the dogs seemed focused on a particular direction, but photos revealed only a couple orbs. Might have had something to do with the coyotes who were watching us the whole time.

3 – Run 2

Our first stop after leaving the East Gate was Run 2 at about 1245 a.m. The dogs were at ease in this location and I didn't feel anything.

4 – Homestead 2

We fought our way past disgruntled cows to get to Homestead 2. Photos of the area around the shack showed some impressive orb counts in one picture. It took us by surprise seeing as how we didn't feel anything unusual.

5 – Homestead 3

The dogs were uneasy at Homestead 3. There was nothing in the photos we took, but we did hear some howling close by.

6 – Investigative Notes

I've never felt so vulnerable in my life then I did last night walking alone in the middle of the desert with coyotes following my dog and myself the whole time and the possibility of confronting a trespasser alone after having heard a gun hot earlier. Needless to say, I had one hand on the leash and the other on my holster

Utah Ranch

Daily Report 090816
Submitted by V/r Robert

Daily Summary of Events:

1. Orb at East Gate
2. Light coming from Tree at Homestead 1
3. Homestead 2 (Robert trying to make contact)
4. Investigating notes

1 – Orb at East Gate

At approximately 2151, while conducting security related duties at the East Gate, Max began to bark and growl. I observed Robert take some photos and in one of the photos he caught one of the brightest orbs I have seen since I have been up here at the ranch. At the time posted at the East Gate, there were no security incidents to report.

2 – Light coming from Tree at Homestead 1

At approximately 2203 while performing security related duties at the East Gate, Robert asked me to come over to where he was standing. Robert stated he is seeing a blinking light coming from the Tree at Homestead 1. As I made it to where Robert was standing, the light had stopped blinking. At approximately 2222, I saw the light in the tree that Robert saw. I called Robert over to show him the light I was seeing and to verify that it was the light he had seen. Robert stated that he could not see the light I was speaking of; I saw the light a second time and Robert stated again he still could not see the light.

3 – Homestead 2 (Robert trying to make contact)

At approximately 0130, Robert and I arrived at Homestead 2. We then begin to set up our chairs. My chair was facing the field to the south; Robert's chair was facing the house at Homestead 2. Robert then began to meditate. After a few moments, he asked me to take some photos. I took several photos and was able to capture several, 100 orbs, to Robert's right. With this experience at Homestead 2, I did not have any bad feeling or feel funny whatsoever.

4 – Investigating Notes

At the East Gate Max showed us that they are starting to pick up on the strong orbs in the area. I am unsure of what to think about the light seen at Homestead 1 by Robert and I, due to the fact when one of us saw the light, the other person couldn't see it. I plan to look into this more when Thomas arrives. The orb activity seems to be picking up finally after all the weird weather we have had the past few days on the ranch.

Deployment to Utah Ranch

Daily Updates: Completing Weekly Report
Day 14 (16 Aug 09) 09/08/16
Submitted by: V/r Robert

Highlights for 09/08/16:

1. Bright Orb (Max starts barking)
2. Light in the Tree (Homestead 1)
3. Meyer sees Light in the Tree (Homestead 1)

4. Homestead 2 (Making Contact)

5. Investigative Note (Going Home)

1 – Bright Orb at East Gate (Max starts barking)

At approximately 2151 while conducting East Gate Security duties, Max began growling and then proceeded to begin barking towards the south field adjacent to the East Gate. I was deeply surprised because Max tends to bark and growl only when dealing with persons who drive up to the gate. I began taking photographs and captured one of the brightest orbs I've seen to date. This is a great sign that the dogs are beginning to pick up on strong orbs in the area; however, this was the first time she had sensed fear or protection of me when an orb has been present.

2 – Light in the Tree (Homestead 1)

At approximately 2203 while performing security duties at the East Gate, I observed between 6 to 8 flashes of light from one location in the large tree located at Homestead 1. The specific location of the light was approximately 20-30 feet up from the center and approximately 4 to 8 feet left in the tree. I immediately asked Mark to look, however as soon as he walked over to me, the light stopped. Note: This was the same location Nick and I observed on day 5 of our trip to the ranch. After Mark walked over, Max began to growl again in the direction both Mark and I were looking. The difference between the first time I saw the light with Nick was the other dogs located at Homestead 1 were not barking this time. Additionally, the wind was not blowing as strong on 090816 as the other time.

3 – Mark see's the light in the Tree (Homestead 1)

At approximately 2222, Mark called out that he too is seeing then light from the large tree located at Homestead 1. I looked, but could not see the light the second time Mark stated he saw the light again. Theory: There is a possibility the light which I saw on two occasions and the light Mark saw with me standing next to him, leads to the possibility this light manifested for some reason beyond our understanding and that we now have three separate eyewitnesses to the same location and under similar circumstances.

4 – Homestead 2 (Making Contact)

At approximately 0100, Mark and I departed Homestead 1 for Homestead 2 to conduct a meditation and attempt channeling with positive entities to create a light in the field. My second focus was to capture one hundred plus orbs in the area which has been impossible since we've had bad weather the past few days. We arrived at approximately 0130 and set the chairs up with Mark facing towards the field (south) and me facing the homes at Homestead 2 (north.) I began mediating and asked for them to create a light in the field, which upon completion, Mark did not see any lights created by my meditation. I did however, ask the spirits to manifest or appear to my right and upon feeling a warm sensation, I asked Mark to begin taking photographs. As seen in the digital photographs, Mark was able to capture hundreds of orbs to my right. I also asked him if any time he felt uneasy or concerned while walking there or while in the area to which he responded, "no." While I'm home, I will continue to work on my channeling and read additional books on the topic. I have confidence with more information and practice I will be able to achieve better results during my time on the ranch in the near future.

5- Investigator Note

Currently, the activity at the ranch has begun to pick up again which is very exciting. However, it is time to go home for a few weeks. The experiences that I have had the pleasure to experience only fuel the desire to continue training and trying new and different techniques. I believe this is a once in a lifetime opportunity to tap into a different world that most of us will never experience. I hope within time our successes will continue and different experiments help prove or disprove certain challenges on the ranch. I'm very eager to take part in many of the tests and efforts in understanding what is going on and how those discoveries can change the outcome for the future.

Utah Ranch

Daily Report
090821
Submitted by: Mark

Daily Summary of Events:

1. Threat heard over the radio
2. Security related duties at the East Gate
3. Homestead 1&2
4. Investigative notes

1 – Security related duties at the East Gate

At approximately 1202, Thomas was sitting on the couch reading "The Hunt for the Skinwalker" and I was on the other couch. While doing this we heard the radio go off on channel 21 (the same channel as last night.) Transmitted over the radio was a verbal threat stating, "I don't know if you can hear me, but I'm going to kill you." Needless to say, I am not very happy about this threat received especially because we patrol alone.

2 – Security related duties at the East Gates

While posted at the East Gate, Thomas and I heard a gunshot north west of the East Gate at approximately 2200. We scanned the area with our NVG's (Night Vision Goggles) with no results in l incidents. Note: the gunshot made me feel extremely uncomfortable because of the verbal threat received earlier via radio.

3 –Homestead 2 & 3

At approximately 0110, arrived at Homestead 2. I didn't feel anything out of the ordinary, couldn't smell anything unusual, and didn't see anything out of place. I took several photos, but once again turned up minimal activity. At approximately 0145, arrived at Homestead 3. The dogs seemed a little on edge, but I think that had to do with all the cows over at the location. Took several photos, scanned with the NVGs, and came up with nothing.

4 – Investigative Notes

The activity at the ranch still seems to be slow, only catching orbs here and there. I haven't felt anything out of place while exploring the Homesteads. We have a coyote issue on our hands out here. The coyotes keep coming in closer and closer at night. The other night they were sitting 15 feet from me. Note: I think the company needs to get encrypted radios for up here so individuals can not hear what we are saying when we are responding to an incident. If we get encrypted radios, I think we should still keep one of the smaller (non-encrypted radios) with us so we can hear if anyone is using them and if they are close to the property trying to make entry.

Deployment to Utah Ranch

Daily Updates
(5 Sep 09) 090905
Submitted by: V/r Robert & Kelly

Patrol/Observations:

1 – The Mesa (Robert)

At approximately 1955, I departed Homestead 1 for the Mesa. I arrived at the top of the Mesa at approximately 2020, at a point over looking Homestead 1 (highest level of activity.) I conducted a look out/observation post from 2020 until 0005 with zero security activity. During this time I had visual over watch of the East Gate and was able to assist

Kelly in early warning of vehicles approaching the East Gate. The only odd activity while I was on the Mesa was on two occasions I felt an extreme warm pocket of air on my right side. Then temp felt at least 80 degrees if not warmer. However, on my left side I felt the normal 60 degree temp. I was unable to take a photograph before then temperature change dissipated.

2 – East Gate (Kelly)

At approximately 2000, I posted then East Gate with K-9/Max. I took numerous photographs, but no anomalies were photographic or noted. Four vehicles approach the gate within ¼ mile, but all turned around and departed before they reached the gate.

3 – Homestead 2 (Robert and Kelly)

At approximately 0300, we both arrived at Homestead to take photographs of the battery test. During our time there, we took digital photographs of the area outside then home, as well as inside the home where the experiment is taking place, and did photograph some orbs; activity level was low to moderate.

At approximately 0339, Robert began to do his meditation/channeling in the middle of the field behind

Homestead 2. While Robert meditated, Kelly took digital photographs of the area as well as Robert, which identified numerous orbs in and around Robert. Furthermore, in one specific photograph that contained many different colored orbs, Bella appears to be looking right at the large presence of orbs.

4 – Dog Run (Robert and Kelly)

At 0400, Robert and Kelly arrived at Dog Run 2 to take photographs and watch the field for an anomalous activity. During our time there, we tried taking some digital photographs without the flash feature to try to capture some orbs. We were unable to identify any orbs, however when we did utilize the flash, numerous orbs can be seen in a few photographs. Additionally, Bella was with us inside the Dog Run and she made no specific change in behavior while there inside the caged area.

5 – Homestead 1 (Robert and Kelly)

At approximately 0430, we arrived at Homestead 1. Both of us took numerous photos, but did not capture any significant activity.

6 – Investigators Notes

a.) Robert's: I believe due to our limited legal rights and current laws in Utah to be obvious to any, it would be trespassing by using a 2 million candle watt light on the top of the Mesa. The best deterrent is our presence and by making ourselves known to local would be trespassers that would attempt to trespass. This also accomplishes officer safety, 1) Able to establish subject actions, 2) Trespassers' potential motives, 3) Appropriate level of action on the security personnel's part on how to deal with the situation after making themselves known to these persons. In closing, this new tactical way of dealing with these persons who have no respect for other people's property, will have a very difficult time in planning trips to the mesa knowing we are actively looking for them. From a liability standpoint, we also help show that due to the risks involved in walking in the area during hours of darkness that our intent is to prevent people from crossing onto the property versus trying to catch them.

B,) Kelly's: None.

Ryan Skinner and Cheryl Carter

Battery Test Experiment, Homestead 2

Date	Time	AA Battery 1.5v	Camera Battery 3.7v	6v Battery #1 (Left Bat.)	6v Battery #2 (Right Bat.)
9/5	11:30	1.274	0.061	6.29	6.27
9/5	19:30	1.268	3.61	6.29	6.26
9/6	3:30	1.238	3.222	6.26	6.24

Weather Notes:

Partly cloudy, approx. 61F, light winds, and overall very pleasant.

Deployment to Utah Ranch

Daily Updates
(7 Sep 09) 090907
Submitted by: V/r Robert and Kelly

Patrol/Observations:

1 - The Mesa (Robert)

At approximately 1948, I departed Homestead 1 for the Mesa. I arrived at the top of the Mesa at approximately 2004, at a point overlooking the land to the north of Utah Ranch property. I remained in the top mesa till 0012 with zero security activity. The only anomalous activity while on the mesa was two lights I observed with my naked eye. One light was due south east and was a very bright white light (appeared much brighter than a vehicle headlight) for just a second and then disappeared. The light resembled a spot light, but possibly brighter due to the distance over two miles. The white light did not appear to move, but just appeared to turn on like a light switch and turn off in the same manner. Due to my location, I was unable to look into the origin of the light. Additionally, I continued to scan the area and was unable to see any additional light for the remainder of my time on the mesa. Due to my elevation, I believe there was no way this light was from a vehicle. I will continue to observe the area of which I observed this light, however, at this time I have no further explanation. The second light I observed was in the area of Bottle Hollow. The light could have been a shooting star, due to a direction due north in what appeared to be a straight line or northerly pattern, however due to some cloud cover the light immediately disappeared after a brief observance. The light was extremely fast (much faster than any aircraft I've ever seen) and did not provide me any time to further assess the incident before the light disappeared behind some clouds north of my position.

2 - East Gate (Kelly)

At approximately 2000, I posted the East Gate with K-9/Max. I took numerous photographs capturing a few anomalies/orbs. No vehicles approach the gate. It was a very calm, quiet night, the only notable observation. Max slept the entire time and the coyotes were not heard howling as normal.

3 - Homestead 2 (Robert and Kelly)

At approximately 0300, we took photographs of the battery test. During our time there we also took digital photographs of the area outside then home as well as inside then home in which the experiment is taking place, and did photograph some orbs; activity level was moderate.

4 - Homestead 1 (Robert and Kelly)

At approximately 0430, we arrived at Homestead 1. We put up the dogs, took numerous photos, and observed Bella rolling in the grass. During this time Robert began taking photographs of Bella and observed one or two orbs in each photograph. Robert was able to continue to observe in his photographs bright colorful orbs in the area.

5 - Investigators Notes

a) Robert's: Activity appears to be picking up with orbs and tonight's light. Security issues have dropped since one week ago. We will continue to maintain low light activity until after 0100 to help calm down possible conflicting views from possible outsiders from an anomalous activity that could be misconstrued as our camera flashes if they are in the area. Further, the cows have been removed from the primary Homestead.

b) Kelly's: None

Battery Test Experiment, Homestead 2

Date	Time	AA Battery 1.5v	Camera Battery 3.7v	6v Battery #1 (Left Bat.)	6v Battery #2 (Right Bat.)
090907	1130	1.081	2.328	06.21	06.18
090907	1930	1.030	2.294	06.21	06.18
090908	0330	0.898	2.151	06.18	06.15

Weather Notes: Scattered clouds, approximately 60F, light winds, and overall very pleasant

Ryan Skinner and Cheryl Carter

Utah Ranch

Daily Updates
(11 Sep 09) 090911
Submitted by: V/r Mark and Kelly

Patrol/Observations:

1 - The Mesa (Mark)

At approximately 2000, I posted the East Gate with K-9/Max in order to assist Kelly with the comparative 35mm/digital photo experiment. I additionally maintained visual surveillance of the eastern end of the Mesa observing the area for any trespassers or anything out of the normal. I did not observe any activities or anomalous/orbs on or around the Mesa.

2 - East Gate (Kelly)

At approximately 2000, I posted at the East Gate with K-9/ Rucca. I took 36 photographs each with the digital camera and the Pentax 35mm camera in the same manner as we did at the East Gate. I captured several anomalies/orbs with the digital camera. We also photographed the battery test.

5 - Homestead 1 (Mark and Kelly)

At approximately 0345, we both arrived at Homestead 1 with K-9/Max and Rucca. We took 11 photographs each with the digital camera and the Pentax 35mm camera in the same manner as we did at the East Gate. I captured some anomalies/orbs with the digital camera. Put up both K-9 Max and Rucca.

6 - Investigators Notes

a) Mark: None

b) Kelly: Approximately 2220, while posted at the East Gate I found a 3x5 index card stuck in the gates chain. The card read: "My name is John. I am the Criminal Investigator for the Ute Tribe. I would like to speak to someone at this residence regarding a particular matter. Please call me at 435-724-xxxx (cell) thank you." Under the impression from the language, John identifying himself as a criminal investigator, we believed that John maybe was acting in an official manner as a BIA police officer. At approximately 2230, we contacted Mr. King, informed him of the situation, what the note said, and requested guidance on whether to respond or not. Mr. King advised us to return his call and determine the nature of the inquiry.

At approximately 2245, I call John (I did not give any personal and/or corporate information of any kind, or acknowledging any of his speculations on who we are or what we do), I simply told him I was responding to his note left on the gate of the ranch, and inquired how I could be of assistance to him. John first informed me that he was in no way acting in an official manner as a police officer, but had some personal concerns of several situations that had been happening at his home which is approximately one mile west of the ranch (approximate location, Independence Road and 4500 East). He heard about "the ranch" in regards to paranormal activities, and possible paranormal investigative operations being conducted here from his co-workers, neighbors, and friends and that he had also did some research on the ranch. He thought we might be interested in his situation/story. He stated that he and his family had moved into their present home in February 09 and since that time they have experienced several unusual situations. He described a situation where he was awoken at about 0200 to the sounds of his children playing in the living room only to find everyone in the house fast asleep. His brother was startled by someone looking in the home's window, but when he went outside to investigate, no one was there. He mentioned something about repeatedly hearing voices of a young girl when there was no one there. Most recently, this week, his wife called him in a panic (approx. 1030) and told him there was a large animal on the barn roof (the roof is approx. 15 feet high), an animal she had never seen before. He asked her if it was a mountain lion or bob cat and she said no. She knows what a mountain lion or bobcat looks like and it wasn't that. She told him that it leaped off the roof and disappeared. She described it as looking like "Smeagol from the movie "Lord of the Rings." John further stated that once he returned home, he investigated the situation, looking for signs of tracks, claw marks, etc, around the barn, but there was none. He relayed that unusual things have been happening at his residence since almost the first day they moved in and that he wanted to know if we (the people at the ranch) would be interested in what was going on.

I informed John that his situation may be of interest and I would pass on his contact information to my heads office, but their normal business hours were Mon-Fri. He then stated he would be out of town on Monday at a conference in Flagstaff AZ, but he would have his cell phone with him. If we couldn't get a hold of him, leave a voice message.

Personal Observation: John's conversational tone seemed sincere. He was very descriptive and concerning. He seemed eager to get our attention.

Utah Ranch

Daily Updates
(8 Oct 09) 091008
Submitted by: V/r Ryan and Cordayo

Patrol/Observations:

1 - East Gate (Ryan)

At approximately 2000, I posted at the East Gate along with K9/Max and K9/Rucca. Shortly after getting there, I took several photos. One of the photos revealed a single white orb. It was clear skies and a little windy when I took the photos. I was sitting by the East Gate observing with my eyes and ears and watching the dogs for anything out of the ordinary. I was sitting in a chair just off the road facing north about 15-20 feet from the gate. The dogs were being unusually calm. At 2137, the dogs both jumped up and started barking at something behind me. I immediately started taking photos. I captured a few anomalies/orbs in the photos and after I stopped taking photos, I saw a single white orb with my naked eyes. It was very bright and about half the size of a golf ball. It was about ten feet from me and was gone after about two seconds. It came into my view from my right. It wasn't moving in a straight line. It was moving up and down erratically. I tried unsuccessfully to get a picture of it. As I was about to take a picture, it vanished just as suddenly as it had appeared. I started to take more photos and then I heard what sounded like a voice. This was only 10-15 seconds after I saw the orb. It was coming from directly in front of me. I couldn't make out any words or how many words. The best way to describe it would be a deep creepy whisper, but it didn't sound threatening at all. At the time I heard the voice, I was standing in the road facing south about 10 feet from the gate. It sounded like a male voice. Immediately after hearing the voice is when I first noticed both dogs were acting very timid and scared. They were both whimpering and curling up against my legs and had their tails between their legs. They continued to act this way for at least another hour. I continued taking photos and captured several anomalies/orbs. I didn't feel any strange emotions nor did I notice any strange odors in the air during the experience. I did, however, get the chills and feel a little freaked out after hearing the voice. I radioed to Cordayo who was at the Mesa with K9/Bella. I told him what I experienced. He decided to walk down to the east gate to investigate with me. Cordayo and K9/Bella arrived at approximately 2155. I told him everything I experienced. We both continued taking photos in all directions. We were able to capture various anomalies/orbs. A few of the pictures captured some unique anomalies that I had never seen up to that point. We continued to scan and take photos in the area of the East Gate and the road leading back to Homestead 1 so we could start the report while the incident was still fresh in our minds. We arrived back to the trailer at approximately 2335.

2 – Mesa (Cordayo)

Approximately 2010, I posted at the Mesa along with K9/Bella. I took my time getting up to the top because of the darkness. When I arrived at the top, I used the NVGs to observe the area for any anomalies/orbs. I couldn't get any photos because of the lack of backdrop. At approximately 2139, Ryan radioed me explaining what he just experienced. I think decided to walk down to the East Gate and investigate with him. I arrived at approximately 2155, asked a few question and started taking photographs. I captured a few anomalies/orbs. At 2335, we headed back to Homestead 1.

3 – East Gate (Ryan and Cordayo)

Approximately 0030, we departed for Homestead 2 with K9/Bella. As we were leaving Homestead 1, we noticed brake lights at the East Gate. When we were about 100 feet away we noticed a blue in color Astro van backed up to the gate. We used NVGs to make sure there was no threat and proceeded to approach the vehicle. We noticed two persons outside the vehicle by the gate. At about 50 feet, a male yelled, "Hey, who are you?" We did not say anything and kept walking towards the vehicle. We shined our flashlights at them and they got back into the van and drove away quickly. Due to the darkness we could not see how many people were in the van. We proceeded to walk to the East Gate and confirm that there were no more persons. We stayed and scanned the area and departed for Homestead 1. On the way back Bella pulled to the left side of the road and tried to get under the fence. We then used the NVGs and noticed a person on the other side running into the woods. We scanned the area and East Gate one more time, but did not see any more persons. We then headed to Homestead 2 with no incidents.

4 – Homestead 2 (Ryan and Cordayo)
Approximately 0200, we arrived at Homestead 2 with Bella. We took a few photos, but did not see any anomalies/orbs. We scanned around and found no signs of trespassers or anything out of the ordinary.

5 – Homestead 3 (Ryan and Cordasyo)
Approximately 0230, we arrived at Homestead 3 with K9/ Bella. Took numerous photos and captured no anomalies/orbs.

6 – Walking back towards Homestead 1 (Ryan and Cordaya)
Approximately 0300, we started walking back to Homestead 1. During the trip back, we took some photos revealing no anomalies/orbs. We didn't notice

any strange odors, temperature change, or strange feelings. K9/Bella was acting normal.

Weather Note: 35 degrees, calm winds, clear skies, 18% humidity

Chapter 5
Incident Reports

Ranch Security Incident Report 090803
Submitted by: C. K.

Incident on Utah Ranch

On the night of 090803, at approximately 2145, Robert Bigelow, CK., Jean Dietz, and JW left the double wide trailer in order to patrol on the path leading to the west end of the ranch. RTB, CK, and JW carried a set of Gen III NVG and assorted cameras. CK carried a Thermal Eye X200 XP thermal imager. Security officers Robert and Nick were stationed with dogs on top of the Mesa and at the East Gate respectively.

All four people arrived down at the small pasture containing the second Homestead and both CK and JW entered the pasture to check activity near the Homestead. Both were stationed about sixty feet from the Homestead and scanning the area with NVGs. Both noticed a large approximately 40-50 pound animal that was moving slowly, almost casually in a northerly direction. RTB and JD were stationed on the path and the large animal was moving slowly in their direction.

Through the NVGs the animal was watched separately by JW and CK and to both observers it appeared to ignore both people as it walked slowly and casually to within 100 feet of both observers. The animal appeared hunched to CK and appeared to have a large amorphous tail, not unlike a beaver tail, although the NVG resolution was insufficient to define.

The animal passed out of view behind the old Homestead still going north and almost immediately, Bella the dog followed it. Bella then reappeared around the house apparently not having encountered the animal. This fact was puzzling since Bella should have encountered the large animal.

Both CK and JW then walked after the animal and searched the tree line carefully, but the animal was not found. The lack of sound of the animal, the casual demeanor, the fact that the animal ignored two nosey observers within 100 feet, Bella's failure to encounter the animal, the failure of both observers to find the animal within a couple of minutes of its disappearance, all combined were judged to be anomalous.
No further anomalous events were encountered that night.

Utah Ranch Dog incident: Addendum 090823
Submitted by: Thomas

This is a summary report of the incident which began on August 23, 2009, in which Max and Rucca, our two black labs, escaped from their runner under what seemed, at the time, to be rather unusual circumstance.

August 23, 2009

Due to periodic rain and the presence of lightning, Mark and I posted out together in the SUV at the beginning of the shift. At about 9:00 PM MST, Mark and I returned to Homestead 1 for water and batteries when I noticed that the dogs were gone. Upon close inspection we were taken aback by the fact Rucca seemed to have just been set free. Max's line was pulled on with such strength that it bent the steel hook that the runner was attached to and the hook connecting the wire to his collar was gone.

We immediately took photos of the runners and the damage caused and swept the immediate area extensively for unfamiliar footprints, but found nothing. We then began a foot sweep of the area from Homestead 1 to the area south of the Run 1 because the cows were discontent, but didn't see the dogs there. We terminated our search for the dogs figuring they would just come back in a few hours; apparently they have a history of getting free and disappearing for a couple hours at a time.

We returned to the East Gate. At 10:00 PM, Mark said he saw a blue LED light coming from the Mesa adjacent to Homestead 1. We expedited back to Homestead 1 and using NVGs and spotlights completed a detailed search of the area, but did not locate anything along the Mesa. Mark could have been mistaken or the individual (s) could have fled the scene in the face of our rapid response. Continued monitoring did not reveal any additional activity in that area. At midnight we left the East Gate enroute to patrol the west side of the ranch when we were ambushed by a very wet and happy duo of Max and Rucca. Max's hook was indeed still on his collar.

August 24 – present
We spoke to Jean and Richard about the incident. They both stated they had not released the dogs from their leads, nor had they heard or seen anyone near the dogs. Jean stated that both dogs had been barking for the past two nights, on both occasions focusing their attention on the area of the Mesa. Over the past three days the dogs have repeatedly shown an

ability to get off their hooks simply by twisting or turning the right away. If one gets off the lead the other does everything they can to get off as well. Mark and I, while feeding the dogs, actually witnessed Max turn to face Mark and his hook came off as easily as if I bent over and released him. Richard has tried much to his frustration to secure the dogs, but they seem to get out every time. We are currently working on solutions to the problem that wouldn't hamper their ability to move around yet secures them to the runner without fail. Ike spoke to us and said he was bringing locks (TSA type) and chock collars to secure the dogs to their leads. Additionally, we are considering bringing them inside the compound on occasion to ensure they do not get away.

Conclusion: It would appear the incident on the evening of 23 August could simply have been Rucca getting free from her lead. After she began running free, Max likely became excited enough to pull himself free. It would not appear anyone with nefarious intentions released the animals.

Chapter 6
That One Time
Ryan Skinner's Escape

One night I was researching with a fellow investigator up along a place locals call Werewolf Ridge which is located to the north of the Ranch. With equipment in hand and adrenaline rising, we quietly trekked across the forbidden landscape in hopes of capturing evidence and also in hopes of not being discovered.

Suddenly, our worst fear was realized as we detected a light coming from behind us that appeared to be approaching quickly. Our adrenaline level lurched momentarily as we both realized we had been discovered and it was most likely the guards coming for us. We had heard stories of people being handcuffed and pepper sprayed before taken back for questioning. There was No way that we were going to experience that!

Quickly deciding it was every man for himself, we took off in different directions. He headed somewhere behind me and I didn't look to see where. Instead, I ran blindly into the darkness as fast as I could even though it seemed almost impossible to escape detection. Jumping down the hill would result with me landing on the Ranch right within everyone's view. I would be trapped within the confines of the gates and at their mercy. No way was that going to happen!

So just up ahead I found a large space between the rocks that seemed suitable for hiding. At least that was what I hoped. I crouched inside making myself as inconspicuous as possible while attempting to squeeze myself deeper into the darkness of the corner in hopes the guard wouldn't see me. Sweat poured down the back of my neck which cooled quickly in the chill of the night air which only contributed to the chills that were running down my spine.

Then the moment of truth soon came to be as I heard the guard approach ... and he had a dog! I began to hear a loud thumping sound, but realized it was only my heart. One loud breath, one heartbeat too many and I would surely be found. I would be handcuffed, interrogated, and probably arrested.

I listened as the dog sniffed around ... closer ... closer they came. I felt like a gambler with a losing hand thinking for sure it was all over for me now. However, for some reason it suddenly got quiet once again. For some reason the dog was unable to pick up my scent possibly because he was not properly trained yet. Then I watched in amazement as they turned around and went back down the trail.

Not wanting to take the slightest chance that the dog might see me or that perhaps another guard would be investigating my whereabouts, I laid low in my hiding place for a few more hours. When I finally felt that the coast was clear, I ran as fast as I could to where we had hidden our vehicles. My friend's vehicle was gone so that must have meant he escaped too. I drove over to his house where I had planned to stay that night to see if he was there.

When I knocked on the door, he motioned me to come in. We were both relieved that we had successfully escaped what we thought was the inevitable. I asked him how he was able to make his escape and he related a crazy story; a crazy story that is priceless.

Instead of hiding, he had taken off through some neighboring property that was familiar to him. However, as he started walking down the road he saw two Police Officers approaching him. Then to make matters worse, as he was standing in front of a house, their dog started barking really loud. Quickly thinking, he looked back at the house and yelled, "Dammit Rocky, why are you barking at the nice Police Officers? Shut up!" ... "Sorry guys, he's always doing that," he said as he opened the random mailbox pretending to look for mail.

"Have you seen any people on the road tonight? We're searching for two trespassers," the officer said.

"No sir, I haven't," he replied.

"Ok well thank you anyway," the officer said. "You have a good evening."

Then my friend casually walked up the driveway of the house until he could see the Police were gone. Then he ran as fast as he could to where his vehicle was hidden and got out of there.

At a later date when I became privy to the following Guard Report, I finally realized just how lucky the "unnamed person" in the report was to escape that night. Surely something on that forbidden trail was protecting him.

BAASS
Utah Ranch Security Incident 09-01

Synopsis:

Robert was able to confirm two unauthorized persons on the Utah Ranch property or the property directly adjoining our property to the north. Upon further investigation, Robert determined the individuals were utilizing light altering devices, which prevent flashlights to be seen with the naked eye. Unfortunately, due to their location, distance to make contact, extra weight (gear), dog, and rough terrain with only NVGs, Robert lost them in the dark of night.

Local law enforcement (BIA and Sheriffs) were contacted and assisted in conducting a northern sweep, however response time was approximately 20-40 minutes after initial contact and sweep began.

Robert was able to secure numerous items left behind, which does include possible finger prints and additional insight into the type of equipment being utilized for unknown purposes.

Narrative:

At approximately 2045, I departed Homestead 1 for the Mesa. I began my patrol with Max and proceeded up to the switch back trail and made it to the top of the Mesa. As I continued on towards a position overlooking Homestead 2 for anomalous activity, I observed a single beam of light shine on a rock at Grid point (N 40' 15.724° W109' 53.421°, elevation 5067 feet.

At approximately 2230 while maintaining a low profile and utilizing my NVGs, I observed a second light in the same area as listed with no apparent concern for concealment. I attempted to locate the light without my NVGs which was impossible and Max made no observation to noise or limited light from their area approximately 1,000 feet higher elevation over looking Homestead 1.

I immediately notified Thomas of the situation via hand held walkie-talkies. I began taking a slow and methodical approach in traversing the terrain up the furthest slope to limit light exposure, noise, and concealment. I reached the ridgeline and began my path east to attempt to block off any path of travel north of the property, however as I approached the area of the grid point listed above, they began moving quickly to remove their selves from an isolated location where they were originally observed, back into the flat Mesa extending for miles north, east, and west.

I immediately challenged both visible persons, however I had a valley between them and I and this allowed them a valuable 30-45 second head start in the dark of night. I observed one male travel in a north easterly direction which I attempted to keep up with. This male appeared to be a white male, 5'10-6'2, shoe size of approximate 12 inch solid tread sole, wore a Carhartt type jacket (heavy weight), brown or green, and had stopped all usage of his light. Additionally, this person used the rocks in the immediate area to either conceal himself or use the odd rock formations as a means to slow me down, due to having to navigate the terrain with a dog unfamiliar with the terrain. The second person was a male; no further information.

I continued to pursue the first male listed with the assistance of my dog, however she did not track, because of lack of training, the person and I found myself lacking a specific direction of travel. I proceeded to take up a location further north of the location where I had observed these two persons and hoped they would make noise traveling past my area with Max.

I waited approximately 25 minutes with no signs or sounds of these persons and proceeded to return to the area to locate tracks to assist me in the direction of travel. Thomas radioed me that I had been off the air the past 40 minutes and he had contacted Jean who in turn contacted the Sheriff's Office who contacted the BIA for immediate response. At the time I had been in radio contact with Thomas approximately 40 minutes after this incident began, both BIA, the Sheriff's Office, and Highway Patrol was on the scene in the area of Homestead 1 to assist. Thomas related the Sheriff's Office was going to conduct a sweep of the area north of our property on the road for any activity. I terminated all assistance due to no known location or direction of travel.

I proceeded to contact Mr. King (DOS) to notify him of the incident and that I had located their exact location and recovered multiple items left behind. Mr. King advised me to secure the area, bag all items for possible fingerprints and DNA if determined to be needed. I requested Thomas to obtain numerous sealable bags and a paper/cardboard box for evidence preservation, and to make his way to my location for evidence collection.

Thomas arrived and I collected the following items from the area believed to belong to the person(s) who were conducting unknown activity on or near the north boundary of the property:

One water bottle with 1/6 full (no label)

One 24 oz. can of Keystone Light Beer (contents at time of collection were still cold, liquid appeared very fresh and 90% full)

One Sure Fire Tactical Lens cover with a flip top

One cigarette butt found in the area (very fresh)

One Lemon Bad Boy Turbo Shot (Instant Energy Boost, empty)

Two Nature Valley Crunchy Granola Bars (Peanut Butter/Oats 'n Honey, unopened)

One Monster Energy Drink (Mean Bean) Note: This item had shown weathering and time in the environments (Internal contents were dry, which makes notice, this position is familiar to a group of individuals.)

Investigative Note:

All items listed above appear with the exception of the Monster Energy Drink to have been introduced into the environment within an hour from the time of discovery. Furthermore, all items were collected using Leatherman pliers to minimize cross contamination. All items will be tagged with time, date, and initials for chain of custody until otherwise destroyed.

After Actions Review of the Event:

1 - Based on the limited boundary, it is highly recommended to obtain a signed statement from the property owner granting authorization for BAASS Guards to conduct patrols on his property as they see fit. Additionally, the letter also authorizes guards assigned to the Ranch the owner's right to detain and approach for the offense of trespassing if caught on his property. A strong possibility of the location of the trespassers was indeed not on our property (no legal rights.)

2 – Due to limited personal and equipment, is advised when determined possible to purchase a set of Thermal Equipment. The outcome may have been different if I had the chance to see their body temperature versus a silhouette. During low levels of light utilization the NVGs are difficult to locate specific detail in very diverse terrain as what we are dealing with.

3 – Take the fight to them! By taking a higher point of observation, we help even the playing field by catching them walking to our location instead of attempting to maneuver roughly 500-1000 feet with gear (30-40 lbs) and a dog in very difficult terrain at night. However, understanding the trade off of one set of eyes now focused on a direction

north of the North and not of the fields. I would like to point out that since my time assigned to security operations at the Ranch, I can only recall one incident where the person located on the Mesa had observed possible anomalous activity.

4 – Radio contact has been addressed previously. However, a key note is that no time did the trespassers appear to have any type of radio monitoring device or a hand held radio to scan local channels for activity. If they had this device, they could have left well before I was within 60 yards of their position.

The items listed above are suggestions to address this type of circumstance in the future. Our Emergency Beacons worked just like they are designed. It allowed Thomas and LE Patrols on the Basin to locate my position over ½ miles away in very rocky terrain. Additionally, as Thomas was bringing up evidence and collected items, he was able to reference the beacon on top of the location I was at with no problem and made excellent time with a strong reference point.

Conclusion of Events:

The events of this evening involving unauthorized personnel on the property north of the Utah Ranch has a profound effect in future outings of possible UFO watchers or people with other motives. Based upon the actions of security, the persons felt comfortable in the environment with their filtered flashlights. They had also prepared to spend at least a few hours which was cut drastically short due to vigilance and proper utilization of issued equipment.

The persons had made many mistakes which tend to lean to lead towards the possibility we are dealing with persons whom live within 40 minutes of the Ranch based upon the day being Monday night at 2230 until known timeframe if not detected. They had beer with them which if conducting a legitimate tactical operation to either test security or the environment would not be an item brought along on an operation.

Additionally, leaving trash, i.e. cigarette butt, water bottle, beer can (which was 90% full) is extremely sloppy operational tactics. Now they did have the Sure Fire filtered lens cap, however, this item can be purchased for $40-60. Although it is doubtful that the trespassers were on Utah Ranch property and more likely on adjacent property, the actions taken during this incident may have a positive effect in deterring local people who are contemplating trespassing on the Utah Ranch.

Once word spreads in the local community that the Ranch security guards have dogs as the fact that I was able to detect both individuals who were using shielded light sources without me being detected will serve warning to locals that security guards have night vision equipment and may be able to catch trespassers. This information may deter future Ranch visits.

Thank you for your time,

Robert

Chapter 7

Kryder Exploration

"We seldom speak of what others find, but often find that of which others speak"

Investigating the Basin

Robert Kryder is the CEO and Founder of Kryder Explorations of New Mexico. Their mission is: To research through adaptive, advanced, scientific methods, and technologies in an effort to explore and procure evidence of the major enigmatic histories and anomalies, while recovering and preserving any physical evidence. With the focus on openly revealing with as much transparency as possible, Kryder Exploration seeks to present the actuality of the world around us: its wonders and truths, in an unbiased manner to all people.

Kryder Explorations conducted an investigation in the Basin on a property a few hundred feet from the southern fence of Skinwalker Ranch. They employed equipment such as the MAZUR PRM8000, KXPD3 Parabolic Microphone,

Trifield TF2 EMF Meter, FLIR Infrared, and Xgen Night Vision camera.

The MAZUR PRM8000 is a handheld Geiger Counter-Nuclear Radiation Monitor with a 0.001-200 mR per hour range. It is used to conduct Ionizing Radiation readings in order to detect Alpha, Beta, Gamma, and X-Radiation levels.

Alpha – Large positively charged particles with two protons and two neutrons.
Beta – Small, high energy, and high speed electrons.
Gamma – No mass electric charge; the same particles as those that represent visible light. However, they contain more energy which in turn allows them to penetrate almost anything. They are able to destroy living cells, cause gene mutilation and cancer.

After digging a hole approximately one foot deep on the hillside of an adjacent property above the southern fence of the Ranch, they began testing. The MAZUR immediately began ramping and declining without a standing field indicating a radiation reading of .600 mSv (milliseviers) per hour. High ionizing radiation attacks the body's cells by producing chemical changes in the cell DNA resulting in abnormal cell growth. According to the readings, they measured enough radiation to cause severe damage and even death.

The International Commission on Radiological Protection's (ICRP) standards:

0 – 0.110 = 963.6 mSv/per year
0.230 = 2014.8 mSv/per year
0.350 = 3066 mSv/per year
0.470 = 4117.2 mSv/per year
0.600 = 5256 mSv/per year

After sunset, they watched through the camera as the ridge was still glowing with residual heat from the day. Then several large beams of light emanated from the ground and into the night sky. On the Xgen Night Vision camera, they watched as the Mesa suddenly lit up.

A short time later on the Thermal camera, they observed volleyball sized blue and orange orbs just on the other side of the fence on the side of the hill. The blue orb began flying erratically around the orange. An anomaly on top of the Mesa lit up on the camera screen. The source was unknown being as it was too high for a vehicle to have driven up there. A few minutes later the anomaly was air born and classified as a UAP, Unidentified Aerial Phenomena. They couldn't conclude that it was actually a UFO.

Next, they employed the KXPD3 Parabolic Microphone mated with the Photon FLIR which uses a parabolic dish-shaped reflector to collect sound waves from a distant source. They detected what sounded like "children" which is often associated with Bigfoot. While walking along the property, upon further examination they came upon what appeared to be a Bigfoot trail. Some foot prints approximately 15-16 inches were found. However, they were not pronounced enough to make a cast. A hair sample was collected from among the prints.

Robert Kryder w/KXPD3 Parabolic MAZUR PRM8000
© Kryder Explorations

TriField Readings
© Kryder Explorations

Digging Into Skinwalker Ranch

Anomaly on the Mesa
© Kryder Expeditions

UAP in the sky
© Kryder Explorations

Bigfoot Track
© Kryder Exploration

Chapter 8
Bill Muldoon Navajo Medicine Man
Shadow People - Bigfoot Skinwalkers

Bill Muldoon is a Navajo Elder and Medicine Man. He claims to work with the United States Government and is familiar with the phenomena of Skinwalker Ranch. I reached out to him seeking answers to some of the many mysteries of the Ranch.

Shadow People

Ryan Skinner: "Bill, what can you tell me about your experience with Shadow People?"

Bill Muldoon: "Most shadow people are drawn to people with gifts. That's what they are interested in. Unless you learn to travel as they do, you will never go where they go. Some things just travel different.

Digging Into Skinwalker Ranch

My dad knows where they travel. He was the one who told me about it. It's in the Eastern Winnemucca Mountains in Nevada. The shadow people, some of them are cool, but most are not. DO NOT EVER go with them. They will ask, but say no. They will try to persuade you with lies. If you go with them, make sure your affairs are in order because you will NEVER be seen again.

They look like fog, clouds, or vapors. I've seen a few mainly at power spots; very few times outside of power spots. But they are all just spirits cruising around and basically harmless. They know a lot of things though. If you can focus enough they will take their true form and speak. And yes, I see them on most nights.

When you use shadow thoughts, this skill is called "shadow walking." Anyone can learn it. Others use dimensional circles, but you have to have one where you want to go. Going through to the other side is pretty easy, but to travel you have to have another circle where you want to travel. Most of the ancient ones use this for their traveling method because while traveling like that, they can't be seen. And if you are seen, the people who saw you think that they just saw a ghost. Now that is where you get some of the ghosts that people see. A word of advice, you don't want shadow people to teach you how to shadow walk. They demand a heavy price for that.

Bigfoot

Ryan Skinner: "Bill, there are reports of people seeing Bigfoot at Skinwalker Ranch. What do you know about it?

Bill Muldoon: "One thing is for sure, DO NOT piss them off! Other than that they are great people to know. I'm still working on their language. It's very hard and fast. But I go and spend 3-4 days a year with a few, a mother, father, and their daughter. I've been seeing them for the past five years now. I met them when I was camping in the Sierras. I had just finished fishing; a pretty good catch, five trout. Well, I saw sitting there with the fire cooking and smelled something really bad. So I went looking for the source.

So as I was I was walking, following the scent, I was looking around. As I was walking I thought, "Probably should have had a flashlight." As I stumbled and fell to the ground, I didn't think much about it and grabbed what I thought was the tree.

And the first thing that popped into my mind is that trees are not hairy. Next thing I know I'm being picked up and mind you I weigh 240. Right after that I was back on my feet. I apologized saying I didn't see you there. And after that I asked if he was hungry and said I have some fish frying at the fire. So as I was walking back to camp he was following me.

Once I got back to camp I turned to ask him how long he has been out there. And holy shit, when I turned around I see a nine foot f*cking Bigfoot. I could tell when he saw the look on my face that he thought it was funny. So trying to be calm I still offered him the fish, beans and rice. He came to the fire, smelled the fish mainly and made like a sign language. I was beside myself. Then he walks away.

About 10-15 minutes later he walked back into my camp, stops, looks at me, and raised one hand out to me like when you try to calm, someone down. And his other arm went out as if he signaled that it was ok. Next thing I know, two more come walking in being very cautious. Then I said hello and asked how they were doing. The father said something, but it was hard to make out.

I offered them to sit and then father came and sat right next to me. Then I reached over, opened the ice chest and pulled out all the fish I caught. I then motioned as to if they wanted it cooked. The father and mother motioned no and took their fish, while the daughter seemed to be fascinated with what I was doing to the fish. So I ripped some of the fish off and ate it. Then I ripped some more off and offered it to her. She said something that sounded like ten words all together.

Then the father nodded and made a grunting sound. The next thing I know the daughter is reaching for my hand, smells the fish, and then takes it and eats it. So then I started cooking one for her. Everyone ate the food and then made their own bed. The father patted me on the head. Then we all went to sleep. The next day I woke up, but they were gone. They did leave me a bunch of berries and nuts. Ever since then I go back every year. It's pretty cool every year we get to spend a day or two together.

Skinwalkers

Ryan Skinner: "Many people have "seen" an old Native man in a red flannel shirt on the Ranch. Do you know anything about him?"

Bill Maldoon: "That's 'Mr. Marcus,' the old Native man that I've seen on the Ranch. He is the oldest medicine man. No one really knows how old he is. What we do know is that he is older than 1,200 years. As the story goes when his body dies he is reborn again. Then in about three months, he's fully grown. He does not need to be birthed from a human, any animal will do. It's said that he does whatever he wants.

NEVER disrespect him in any way, shape, or form. If anything, offer him tobacco as a peace offering. If he accepts the offering, he will leave you something.

Chapter 9
Somewhere In the Skies
The Basin Speaks

In 1966, Dr. Frank Boyer Salisbury, a Utah State professor wrote an article called "The Scientist and the UFO." Following a presentation he did for the Association of Utah Science Teachers, he was approached by Joseph Junior Hicks a junior high school teacher.

Ever since Hicks and a group of his students saw a UFO flying overhead while they were outside in 1951, he had been investigating a wave of high strangeness and UFO sightings in the Basin area and wanted to share his information. This piqued Dr. Salisbury's interest and he published his book in collaboration with Hicks and based upon his files called "The UFO Display Book: A scientist brings reason and logic to over 400 UFO sightings in Utah's Uintah Basin."

THE SCIENTIST AND THE UFO

Frank B. Salisbury • Utah State University

Dr. Salisbury and Junior Hicks 1952

Junior Hicks at Skinwalker Ranch

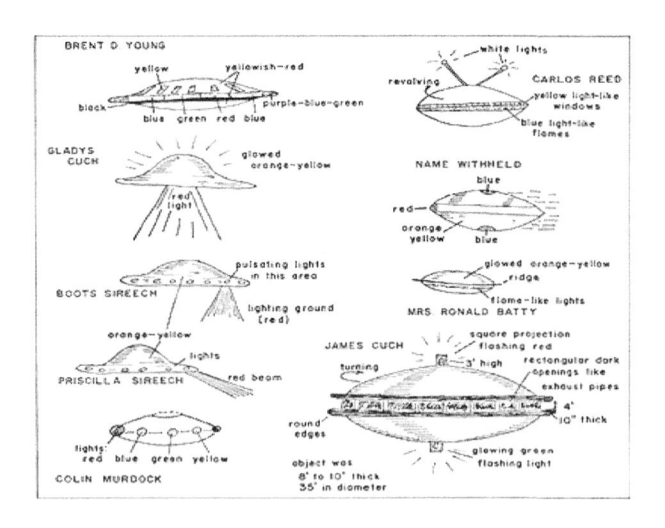

Drawings of various UFO shapes
by witnesses in the Uintah Basin

Digging Into Skinwalker Ranch

> "Intelligence from outer space may be using the Uintah Basin as a UFO base," said the National Enquirer in Lantana, Florida. The newspaper clipping dated September 8 was headed "Atomic Energy Commission Scientist Says Earth is Being Visited By UFOs that May be Using Isolated Area of Utah as a Base." Dr. Frank B. Salisbury says he reached this astonishing conclusion after an investigation of 70 reports of UFO sightings in the remote Uintah Basin area of Utah since 1960.
>
> "I've found 300 witnesses to the Utah sightings, and it would be easy to double that," Dr. Salisbury stated. "There are only 4,000 people in the Uintah Basin, so that's about 15 percent of the local population who have had UFO experiences."
>
> Dr. Salisbury says he believes the Uintah Basin is a UFO base because "this is a desert and mountainous region with tremendously isolated areas." He added, "The sightings in the Uintah Basin are typical of what's been happening all over the world for many years. UFOs show up in a given area for awhile, then disappear."
>
> Dr. Salisbury, who's a member of the Enquirer's Blue Ribbon Panel on Unidentified Flying Objects and author of the book, "A Scientist Looks at UFOs", went on to state, "I think the evidence from my

The newspaper clipping from September 8 was titled "Atomic Energy Commission Scientist Says Earth is Being Visited By UFOs that May Be Using Isolated Area of Utah as A Base." Dr. Frank B. Salisbury says he reached this astonishing conclusion after an investigation of 70 reports of UFO sightings in the remote Uintah Basin area of Utah since 1960.

Dr. Salisbury says he believes the Uintah Basin is a UFO base because "this is a desert and mountainous region with tremendously isolated areas." He added, "The sightings in the Uintah Basin are typical of what's been happening all over the world for many years."

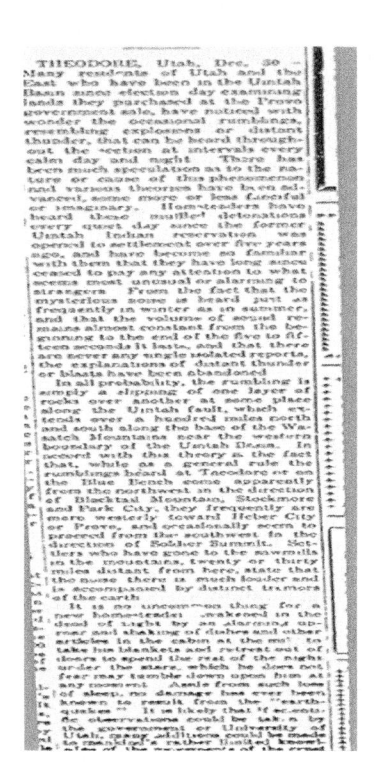

News Advocate 5 January 1911
Strange Rumblings Underground

The locals were hearing explosions and rumblings underground. No one knew what caused it. Was it aliens or the government boring tunnels?

UFO sighting made

The UFO's that caused so much comment several years ago are again being sighted in the Uintah Basin. Approximately eight people reported sighting a single UFO Tuesday morning at approximately 6 a.m.

W. L. TULLIS, 3450 W 2500 N, Vernal sighted the UFO as he got up to close his window. He stated that he watched it as it appeared on the eastern horizon and saw it travel across the valley, disappearing up the Lapoint road. It looked like a ball of fire and was in torpedo shape. It appeared to be about 2,000 foot high and he did not hear any noise from the object.

Tex Ross, 142 S 200 E, said when he first sighted the UFO he thought it was a meteorite because of the long fiery tail trailing it, but after observing it decided that the way it was traveling it was not a meteorite. This is not the first UFO Mr. Ross has sighted. He noted about 10 years ago in the Book-cliff area he and some companions sighted something that was on the same order of the UFO seen Tuesday.

OTHER observers described the UFO as being a cigar shaped "bubble" type flying object which had a bright light in front and a red streak (similar to a jet stream) behind it and at times appeared to be an emerald green. It made no noise that anyone could hear. The UFO was reported as being seen in the Roosevelt area also.

<u>Vernal Express October 1950</u>
Eight people, in the nearby town of Vernal east of the Ranch, observed a cigar-shaped craft in the sky.

Flying Saucer Takes A Look At Oil Basin

RANGELY—Flying saucers are visiting nearer home with the report by seven members of a pipeline crew working for Guy Fox in the Oil Basin that they saw "a shining aluminum colored object hover for more than a minute over the Basin, then move off rapidly to the east."

The observers agreed that it was a "flat, disc-like object which seemed to rotate as it hovered and on top had a dome-like structure."

They said that at regular intervals a flash seemed to come from the object, which may have been flames from an exhaust.

Critics said that an airplane had landed and taken off at the same time that the "saucer" was seen. The observers ridiculed this suggestion saying they were positive it was not a plane they had seen. They said that there was no noise at all heard from the object.

Observers included: Guy Fox, E. G. Painter, John Smith, Lavon Horrocks, Joe McMullen, Doc Rasmussen and Joe Shell.

Mr. Fox estimated the altitude of the object at about 2,000 feet.

The clear blue morning sky rules out the possibility of a reflection from a cloud causing an optical illusion.

Students Sight 'Flying Saucer' Over Duchesne

Flying saucer excitement stirred Duchesne Wednesday when nearly 100 students of the Duchesne elementary school reported watching a silver-colored, disc-shaped object, on Tuesday.

The students, mostly fifth and sixth graders, were in general agreement as to the description of the craft.

Principal Stone had the children draw sketches of the "saucer" on the blackboard. "They coincided to an amazing degree," he said.

The object was described as resembling two saucers placed face to face, when moving in a horizontal position. It was reported as being bright and glistened in the sunlight.

According to the students, the object flew along slowly, going northeast. It hovered in a vertical position, "wavered" a little, sped off at a terrific speed, hovered again, then took off again over the horizon with a burst of speed.

There was no estimate of height, size or speed of the object.

A short time previously, six members of a geophysical crew reported watching a similar "flying saucer," through a surveying instrument in the Duchesne area.

<u>Vernal Express Nov. 30 1950</u>
Seven men, nearby the town of Rangely, working on the pipeline saw a metalic object.

<u>Uintah Basin Standard 1959</u>
100 students, in the nearby town of Duschense west of the Ranch, watched a silver disk shaped object in the sky.

Ryan Skinner and Cheryl Carter

OR WHAT WAS IT
Sunday afternoon about 4 o'clock Mrs. Earl Van Tassel looked out of her big living room window and noticed a brilliant redish object hanging (the word hanging is used, as that is the impression it gave) above Tabby Mt. Flying Saucers were the first thing that came to mind. She called the neighbors and a good percentage of Tabione citizenry as well as many out of town deer hunters saw the same thing. As the sun set it became less redish and glowed like a big diamond in the sky.
With the binoculars its shape could be distinguished as a balloon of some type, evidently a weather balloon. It hung high in the air above Tabby Mt. from 4 o'clock on as people watched it and was the talk of the evening.
It was last seen about 10 o'clock that night in the same spot, high in the sky and brighter than any of the stars.

Strange Objects Descend On Whiterocks Bench ..
WHITEROCKS—Two weeks ago 2 residents of the Whiterocks area had almost identical experiences with two strange gadgets that were released from Army airplanes as they flew over that part of the Basin.
Wednesday morning a note from Fern Houston, our Bennett correspondent, came to the Standard office telling of the experience of Ray Houston, who on his way to his farm to feed cattle on Whiterocks bench, discovered a balloon about 6 ft. in diameter hovering near the ground. Upon examining the gadget, he discovered a radio attachment had been assembled to the balloon, and could be heard.
Only a short time after receiving Mrs. Houston's note, the Standard had a visitor—Mrs. Barbara Wilkerson—who not only told a similar story, but had the funny little gadget in her possession, which had the following identification plate attached to the radio contraption:
—Serial
U. S. Army—Signal Corps—Serial No. 30102; Radio Transmitter T60/ANT-2," and was apparently made by the Automotive Mfg. Corp. No address listed.
Mrs. Wilkerson related that on this particular day, (she couldn't remember the exact date), she had just stepped from her home and was going to feed her chickens when she heard a plane overhead. She looked up just as the Army aircraft, which was flying very low, released the balloon and it floated to earth, landing in her yard. She immediately took possession of the gadget, at least after she had convinced herself it was not a Communistic bomb, and then began wondering just what procedure she should use in publicising her find. Her local newspaper was the final answer.

Uintah Basin Standard
26 October 1961
Reddish object in the sky observed in several towns surrounding the Ranch that remained stationary from 4:00-10:00.

Roosevelt Standard
28 December 1961
Three people in Whiterocks just north of the Ranch, witnessed planes dropping balloons with electronic equipment attached.

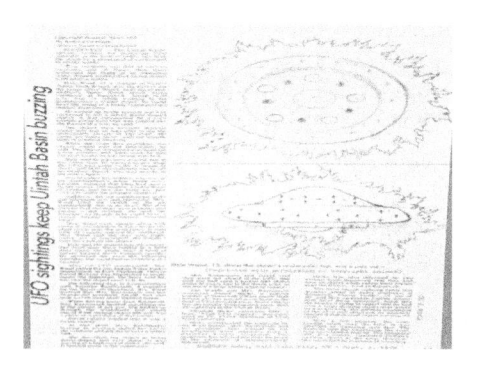

Deseret News 4 September 1978
Witness drawings of strange glowing crafts in the sky near Skinwalker Ranch

Chapter 10
Utah UFO Statists

Cheryl Costa is a native and resident of Upstate New York who had her first UFO experience at age 12. She is a retired information security professional from the aerospace industry. She is the co-author of "UFO Sightings Desk Reference: United States of America 2001-2015." Linda Costa is a retired scientific researcher from Washington D.C. and also resides in New York.

Cheryl and Linda combined the 2018 data from the Mutual UFO Network (MUFON) and the National UFO Reporting Center (NUFORC) and used latitude measurement. Their findings concluded that there are ten other latitude parallels in the United States that have many more UFO reported sightings than the infamous 37th Parallel.

The 34th latitude is number one in UFO sightings. The 40th latitude is second and one particular GPS coordinate is very interesting ... 40°15'29N 109°53'18W

... Skinwalker Ranch.

Skinwalker Ranch 40°15'29N 109°53'18W

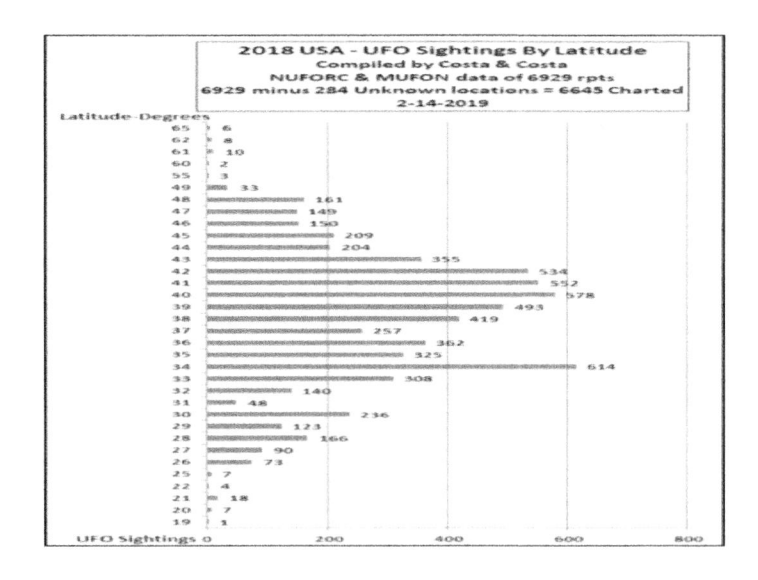

© Cheryl Costa and Linda Costa
UFO Sightings by Latitude

According to statistics gathered by Cheryl Costa and Linda Costa, from 2001-2020, Uintah County hosted 33 sighting reports, ranks 10 of out of 30 in Utah, and ranks 936 out of 2919 counties nationwide.

The top ten shapes include:

- Light – 165, 14.25%
- Circle – 131, 11.31%
- Sphere – 119, 10.28%
- Unknown – 114, 9.84%
- Triangle – 102, 8.81%
- Other – 91, 7.86%
- Fireball – 82, 7.08%
- Disc – 68, 5.87%
- Star-like – 46, 3.97%
- Oval – 38, 3.28%

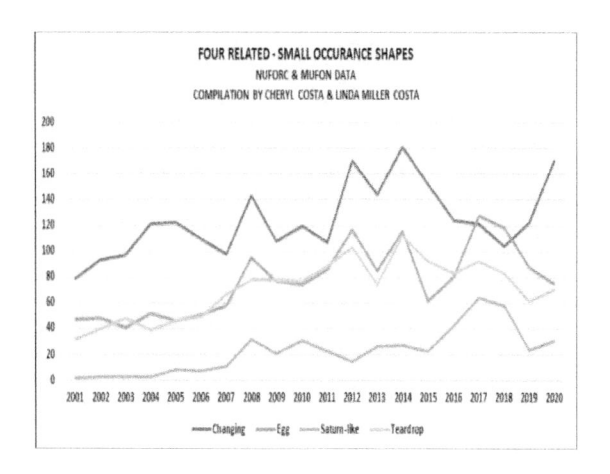

© Cheryl Costa and Linda Costa
Four Related Small Occurrence Shapes

- Changing *stealth craft*
- Egg *small scout craft*
- Saturn *Mother Ship mile wide*
- Teardrop *shuttle*

Top shapes relevant to Utah among the 1158 sightings include:

- Light – 165
- Circle – 131
- Sphere – 119
- Unknown – 114

- Triangle – 102
- Other – 91
- Fireball – 82
- Disc – 68
- Star-like – 46
- Oval - 38

Interesting note: On a map, Skinwalker Ranch forms a Triangle with two other well-known UFO hotspots, Roswell, New Mexico and Area 51 which is located in southern Nevada near Groom Lake. The Ranch is 700 miles northwest of Roswell (33°23'14"N 104°31'41"W) and 500 miles from Area 51 (37°14'0"N 115°48'30"W).

Chapter 11
Utah UFOs
Official MUFON Report
Witness Sightings

MUFON stands for Mutual UFO Network. UFO, an unidentified flying object, is any aerial phenomenon which cannot be immediately identified or explained. The word has become synonymous with any extraterrestrial spacecraft. www.mufon.com

It was founded May 31, 1969, with its sole mission being "The Scientific Study of UFOs for the Benefit of Humanity." MUFON Headquarters is located in Cincinnati, Ohio just 54 miles from the infamous Wright-Patterson Air Force Base in Dayton. This is where it was rumored to be a secret base where aliens from the 1947 Roswell UFO crash were taken to study ... Coincidence?

Digging Into Skinwalker Ranch

Witness Reporting Data Base

Reported by: Roger Marsh
MUFON Director of Communications

MUFON Case #11138

Date: 4 September 2020
Time: 5:15 a.m.
Place: Fort Duchene, Utah

For almost two hours, we watched as two plasma-type crafts flew in and hovered over Skinwalker Ranch. They continued to hover and move around while pulsating and changing shapes. They turned into many different types of shapes.

Distance: 20 feet or less
Altitude: Unknown
Duration: 01:30:00
Features: Dome, patterned surface, other unknown
Flight Path: Hovering then path
Shape: Other
Weather Details: Unavailable

MUFON Case #94603

Date: 1 September 2018
Time: 9:00 p.m.
Place: Duchesne, Utah

My wife and I were camping in the forest. As I was lying down, I first noticed a bright object in the shape of a slightly flattened cross above me. Instantly one of the shapes seemed to flicker from point A to point B and back again. I blinked because I first thought I was not seeing it correctly.

Then it started doing circles in the sky and would shoot from one direction to the next covering great distances at a time. When it would start, other ships would approach it that looked like lightly lit stars. I could then see when two of them got parallel together it would cause a black beam between the two of them. Then the ground would be as though somebody instantly kept changing the light from on top off. It was very dark on the ground almost to the point you could not see your hand. It appeared to me and my wife and one other witness there must have been twelve different objects in the sky moving around in different directions.

Distance: Over 1 Mile

Altitude: Over 500 feet, no cloud cover

Duration: 01:00:00

Features: Unknown

Flight Path: Path with directional change

Shape: Other

Weather Conditions: Unknown

MUFON Case #94215

Date: 6 August 2018

Time: 12:00 a.m.

Place: Fort Duchesne, Utah

Three of us were camping in the Ashley National Forest approximately 25-30 miles away from Skinwalker Ranch. At the time of the event all three of us were set up to look at the sky in hopes of catching something strange with our binoculars and night vision cameras. At about 10:00 p.m. we noticed something right over our heads. It was clearly the brightest and biggest object in the night sky. We thought at first it was a plane, but with the fact that it was not blinking or making a sound, we quickly ruled that out. It moved right over our heads in a straight line path, but seemed to speed up after we shined high powered lasers at it. After speeding up, it headed in the direction of Skinwalker Ranch and slowly dimmed itself out. The entire sighting lasted about 1 minute and 30 seconds and was captured on night vision camera.

Distance: 501 feet to 1 mile
Duration: 00:01:30
Altitude: Over 500 feet, no cloud cover
Flight Path: Path with directional change
Shape: Oval
Temperature: 73° F
Visibility: 10 miles
Weather Conditions: No abnormal weather conditions

MUFON Case #93407

Date: 16 July 2018
Time: 11:41 p.m.
Place: Vernal, Utah

I was out shooting the night sky again. At 11:41 p.m. caught this overhead from Vernal, Utah, pointing almost straight up, slightly northeast. Zooming in at 300 mm caught this in two frames. I am uploading the full image and zooms of each one. You can see the structure in these two images.

Nikon D5200

Lens: 18.0-300.0 mm f/3.5

Exposure: 1.0 sec/ f/16, IOS 100 manual

Distance: Over 1 mile

Altitude: Over 500 feet, no cloud cover

Duration: 00:00:10

Features: Unknown

Flight Path: Path with directional change

Shape: Other

Weather Conditions: Unknown

MUFON Case #69712

Date: 24 July 2015

Time: 3:30 p.m.

Place: Duchesne, Utah

My daughter (36), myself (54), and a male friend (41) went to my property to camp over a four day weekend starting on Thursday July 23, 2015, with two other people both males for a total of five of us. On Friday the 24th, it was very hot about 98-100 degrees. We had planned a hike in a nearby canyon, 10-15 miles away by dirt road by UTV travel, but do to the heat only three of us decided to go on the hike. My daughter and I drove in our UTV and the friend road off on his moto bike. We lead the way and he followed about a ¼ mile behind us do to the road dust.

We hiked until 3:00 p.m. and headed back to camp. Three miles into heading back the friend passed us and went ahead. As we are moving along at around 20-25 MPH my daughter said, "Stop, Dad, stop, stop!" I stopped in just a few seconds as she said, "What is that? What is that?" I leaned back in my seat looking over at her looking up at the ridge top. At first I didn't see anything, but then as I leaned back further and looked forward … there it was.

It was a crescent shaped craft hovering just above the ridge. It was translucent white and curved down to a sharp point on both ends. It hovered for about ten seconds and then started to descend down behind the ridge. As it did, it started to glow very brightly in an orangish earth toner color. There were pine trees spaced out right on the ridge top and it was at least 6-8 trees wide, I'm guessing 150-200 feet wide.

It went down behind the ridge out of sight. As we sat there looking to see if it would come back up, my daughter said it was slowly moving along the ridge top in the same direction we were traveling when we stopped.

It stopped its forward motion and just hovered. That is at the point I saw it, as it was just hovering. We stayed there about 10-15 minutes and didn't see it come back up so we moved on. As we went up the road we saw our friend on his moto bike waiting on the side of the road waiting for us to catch up. He asked us what took us so long and we told him what happened.

Back at camp my daughter was very upset and did not talk much over the next four hours. The area this happened in does not get many visitors. In fact, we did not see any one else the whole day going on our hike or on our way back. The canyon we were in has high walls on both sides of the road. This area I know very well and don't need maps to get around.

Distance: 501 feet to 1 mile
Altitude: Treetop
Features: Dome. Other
Flight Path: Path and then hovering
Shape: Other
Temperature: 74°
Visibility: 10 miles

Weather Conditions: No abnormal weather conditions

MUFON Case #59046

Date: 2 August 2014
Time: 12:00 a.m.
Place: Ouray, Utah

I was at work about 30 miles southeast of Ouray, Utah. In the sky just above the horizon to the northeast of me about a quarter mile away, I noticed a large black object changing shape. It was changing from a sphere to a bird-like form to a pole-like object.

I grabbed my phone and took a couple pictures, but it seemed a little too far away to see very well. I continued watching it change shapes. Then it broke into hundreds of little spheres, just dissipated, and scattered in all directions.

Distance: 501 feet to 1 mile
Altitude: 500 feet or less
Features: Unknown
Flight Pattern: Other
Shape: Sphere
Weather Conditions: No abnormal weather conditions

MUFON Case #71769

Date: 10 February 2013
Time: 1:30 a.m.
Place: Vernal, Utah

On February 10, 2013, at about 1:30 a.m. my son and I were in my driveway installing a stereo in my Durango. In the fields across from our property, we noticed the coyotes, a very large pack of them. Then we heard several growls from something unknown and the coyotes began to call to each other. Suddenly all Hell broke loose because it seemed that whatever was howling was now attacking the coyotes and tearing them apart. It was very, very loud and terrifying to listen to. After it ended, my neighbor came out and asked us what the Hell that it was. We told him we had no idea what just attacked the coyotes. We all went into the woods to see, but felt a terrible fear that we shouldn't be there so we turned around and went home.

The next evening, it was raining a lot. I had several friends over and told them of what we heard the night before. I decided to take them outside to show them about where is happened. Just as I was explaining more, we noticed red glowing eyes staring right at us. I hit them with a laser pointer and then from behind the first being, four and the six more stepped out from behind it. They began jumping and frolicking about each other, while all the time the first one held its stare on us. Then I noticed that two on each side started walking to the side of the field and I was certain they were hunting us. So we tried to gain our flanks and ran back to our house. We watched and waited several hours, but all through the night whatever it was remained there still staring at my house.

The next day they were gone. However, we could not find any footprints which was crazy as it had rained all night. When we measured to the height of the red eyes, they were about ten feet tall. After that I had several strange events. Strong, floating orbs in the sky above my house. One night my son, a friend, and I witnessed one of the flashing lighted crafts land in the mountain range just above my home. One night something spooked my dogs. It was a terrible whooshing sound like giant wings followed by a jet-like explosion that blew through my yard in a south direction. Something picked up the tree in my backyard that had fallen, turned it 180 degrees, and then sat it down with no markings from it ever being moved from the Earth.

Distance: 101 to 500 feet

Altitude: Landed

Features: Unknown

Flight Path: Path and the hovering

Shape: Sphere

Temperature: 18° F

Visibility: 8 miles

Weather Conditions: Snowing

MUFON Case #5136

Date: 26 June 2008

Time: 12:00 a.m.

Place: Vernal, Utah

On June 26, 2008, my wife and I were headed west on Route 40 from Craig, Colorado, top Vernal, Utah. We were entering a valley with mountains on the horizon when I saw to my left, south, at 11:00 p.m. a flash similar to a reflection from a bright metallic object. The object then flew in front of us following the road leading west. At this time, it was ¼ to 1/21 mile away from us and several feet from the valley floor.

It stayed its course for a short period of time and then flew off to the southwest at an incredible rate of speed. When I first saw the reflection and then the object, I was sure I was seeing a reflection on the glass so I moved my head. Now I observed that the object was clearer. I went through every explanation I could think of for what I was seeing, but it became evident that what I observed was a metal, polished, stainless steel type of craft that resembled two saucers placed together one upside down on top of the other. It was near enough too that I could see the middle separating the two ovals. This is not to say that it was a stripe or any such marking, as there were none, but it was the metal line that indicated where the two parts of the saucer were joined.

I saw the object from a number of different positions so I am quite certain as to what I saw. It didn't appear to be spinning, but could have been. The most pronounced feature was its incredible velocity.

Distance: 501 feet to 1 mile

Altitude: Unknown

Features: None

Flight Pattern: Straight line path; path with directional change

Shape: Disc

Weather Conditions: Unknown

Chapter 12
Utah UFOS
Official NUFORC Report
Witness Sightings

NUFORC stands for The National UFO Reporting Center. It was founded in 1974 with its sole mission being "Dedicated to the collection and Dissemination of Objective UFO Data." NUFORC Headquarters is located in Davenport, Washington. In addition to record keeping, the center provides statistics and graphs. www.nuforc.org

Witness Sighting Report Index

Occurred: 4 September 2019

Location: Vernal, Utah
Shape: Circle
Duration: 30 minutes

A bright object was observed over Dry Fork Canyon, Utah:

As my wife and I were doing astro-photography, I realized there was a light in front of us that looked like a bright flashlight moving. I grabbed my binoculars to see who or what it could be. I the realized the light was well above the top of the canyon. The light was brighter than the rest of the stars I was photographing. It moved up and down and side to side at a high acceleration rate. I initially thought it could be a drone, but after seeing the terrain and examining the video I captured I do not think a drone can do what I witnessed the object doing. The video shows the object spinning on its own axis.

Occurred: 13 March 2012

Location: Fort Duchesne, Utah
Shape: Egg
Duration: 8-10 minutes

Glowing egg or oblong shaped flying object rose up from the ground and went west:

My wife and I just put our kids to be. We went outside on our front porch for some fresh air and were just about to go back inside and to bed. We saw a funny light moving slowly up from a low area on the landscape. We live right by the Ute Indian Reservation.

It started changing colors from the steady yellow glow to all kinds when it passed directly over our heads and slowed to no more than 25 mph. As it shifted from color to color, the only sound was a slight buzzing that my wife said she heard. It went away towards the direction of the east I'd say and then maybe 1000 feet away it vanished in the black night sky. At the same time, the power went off all over the area.

Occurred 3 June 2003

Location: Vernal, Utah

Shape: Flash

Duration: 30 minute

There were strobing lights that were stationary, then appeared to take off, and fly away in a faster speed than possible:

As we were driving west toward Vernal on U.S. 40, we saw a flashing light that looked like it was perhaps an airport beacon. It flashed at a regular pulse. It was very bright white with a bluish tone. It flared out into a geometric, multi-pointed, three dimensional star shape. I could see it for several miles as we approached. It was stationary until we were a hundred yards away. Then as it flashed it reappeared to the north and it kept going gradually higher and right more quickly. It accelerated at a slow to faster pace and then turned upward and west blurring in its speed into disappearance. There were empty fields and nothing else in the area that could have caused the lights.

Occurred: 11 September, 1999

Location: Vernal, Utah

Shape: Chevron

Duration: 5-6 minutes

Pilots at local airport watched unidentified craft for several minutes:

At dusk this evening, several pilots, myself included, watched a mysterious craft. I had just landed about 10 minutes before the sighting. The air was relatively calm with a building of some very large dark clouds to the northeast. I had just rolled my plane into the hanger when we heard other pilots talking about what they were seeing. I immediately went outside and observed a craft that appeared to be dark or black in color. It was first thought to be an ultra-light, but appeared to be too large.

Darkness was rapidly closing in and no pilot without any lighting would continue to fly. We kept listening for engine noise, but there was not so much as a whisper. We watched as it approached bearing about 080 degrees, at less than ¾ of a mile it turned to about 360 degrees.

Our consensus was that it was about 1500 AGL, and moving at about 35-40 Kts. As it banked north, it was under the clouds, but mostly obscured by a dark background. Eventually, it came back into clear sky, but had gained altitude, at least another 1000 feet or more. At this point with the darkness and distance, we lost sight of it.

I got a chance to see it with binoculars. It appeared to be chevron shaped. In discussing the incident with the other pilots, we thought that the dimensions of this thing would have a cord of about 6-10 feet and a span of approximately 30-

Ryan Skinner and Cheryl Carter

Chapter 13
Mysterious Crop Circles

Crop circles are large geometric and circular patterns of flattened crops most often found in fields. Some who have studied them believe them to be binary code messages from intelligent extraterrestrial beings. The Independent Crop Circle Researcher's Association, ICCRA, is a team of researchers that studies the various complexities and aspects of the crop circle phenomenon. www.iccra.org

Its founder, Jeffery Wilson, was a member of the Center for Crop Circle Studies, CCCS, in both the United States and United Kingdom. His research has been covered in numerous newspapers and he has been frequently interviewed by Linda Moulton Howe as well. He has a Masters from Eastern Michigan University. He received a grant for his thesis from NASA under the Michigan Space Grant Consortium in order to analyze and map geologic reflectivity data from NASA's Lunar Prospector Mission.

Digging Into Skinwalker Ranch

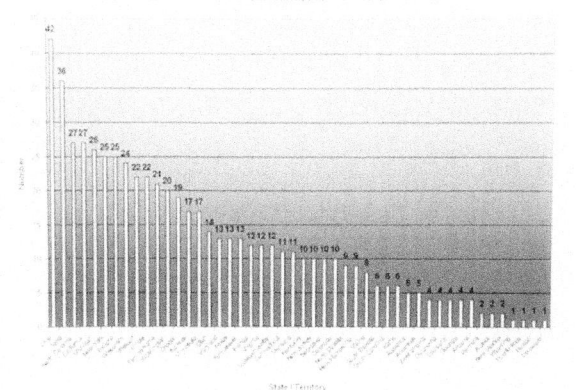

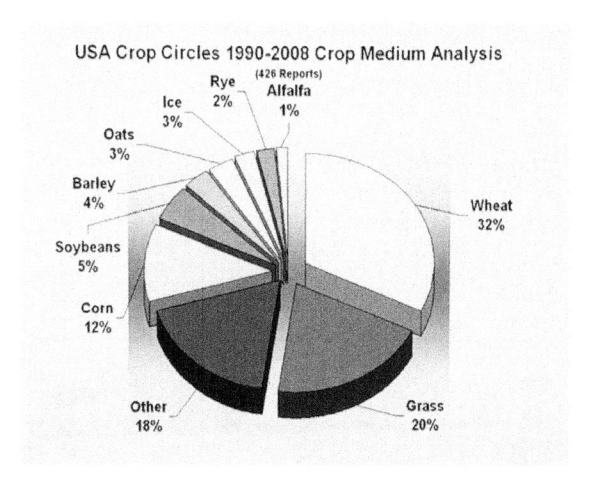

USA Crop Circles 1880-2008 Reports by State / Territory

USA Crop Circles 1990-2008 Crop Medium Analysis (426 Reports)

- Wheat 32%
- Grass 20%
- Other 18%
- Corn 12%
- Soybeans 5%
- Barley 4%
- Oats 3%
- Ice 3%
- Rye 2%
- Alfalfa 1%

Utah – 17 Reports

Fort Duchesne, Uintah County – 1995

Land owners Terry and Gwen Sherman discover a single (size undetermined) flattened, swirled circle in the pasture grass sometime after the beginning of April, 1995. Later that year, they found three eight foot diameter circles flattened in their pasture grass spaced evenly about thirty feet apart in a triangle.

During the year 1995, they observed several different colored balls of light flying around their farm, and in three separate instances discovered three cattle mutilations on their property.

Crop Type: Grass
Source: Deseret News, June 30, 1996

1996 AP photo

Bigelow Ranch, Fort Duchesne, Duchesne County, Uintah Basin – February 21, 2002

A single ice circle was discovered at approximately 7:00 a.m. that was approximately 5'9" in diameter. The circle was located on an irrigation canal in ice that was only ¾ of an inch thick. The circle appeared to be scoured into the ice only ¼ of an inch deep and did not go all the way through the ice, leaving shavings around the circumference of the circle. The circle was cut counter-clockwise. There was no central hole or markings inside the circle.

Crop Type: Ice

Source: Jeffery Wilson

Ice Circle Bigelow Ranch

Ice Circle Bigelow Ranch

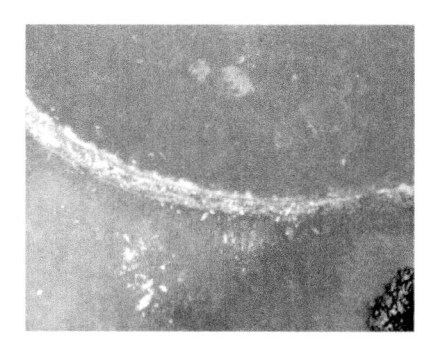

Ice Circle Bigelow Ranch

Spanish Fork, Utah County, June 27, 2004

There was an approximately 200 foot formation in barley, with small circles ranging from 11-31 feet in diameter. The circles were slightly elliptical and their swirled centers were off center.

Digging Into Skinwalker Ranch

There are reports of witnesses seeing balls of light and aerial light phenomena around the time of formation. Some local workers reported their dogs cried for hours then night before the formation was discovered. Electro-magnetic effects and electronic equipment failure was reported. The flattened lay of the wheat was reported to be completely even all the way across the whole of the formation. BTL, Inc, reportedly had soil and plane samples collected.

Crop Type: Barley
Source: Linda Moulton Howe, Earthflies.com

Smithfield, Cache County, Utah – July 6, 1997

Where this formation appeared, a buzzing/beeping sound was heard by residents of the farm the previous night. The larger circle was 75 feet in diameter; the smaller circle was 31 feet in diameter. Electro-magnetic effects were reported.

Crop Type: Wheat
Source: Jeffery Wilson

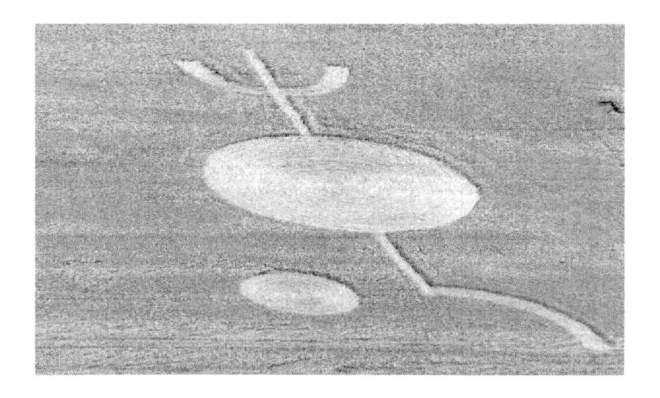

Richmond, Cache County, Utah – July 7, 1997

Around midnight, a sound described as a cross between a buzz and a hum and a beeping was heard by residents living across the street the night before the formation was discovered. The formation was close to 300 feet long. Electro-magnetic effects were reported.

Crop Type: Wheat
Source: Jeffery Wilson

Logan, Cache County, Utah August 23, 1996

This 240 foot long dumbbell-type formation was discovered by a farmer after his tractor broke down and he was walking through the field to get help. The large circle was 85 feet in diameter; the smaller circle was 40 feet in diameter. The formation was not visible from anywhere outside the field. Balls of light were reported being seen in the formation later.

W.C. Levengood reported node length expansions, expulsion cavities, altered soil structures determined by x-ray crystallography conducted by geologist Diane Conrad-Gleason, reduced seed weights, and seedling growth from formation plants.

There were reports of a squadron of black, unmarked apache helicopters over the field just a few days before the formation was discovered by the farmer.

Crop Type: Wheat
Source: W.C. Levengood and Diane Conrad-Gleason

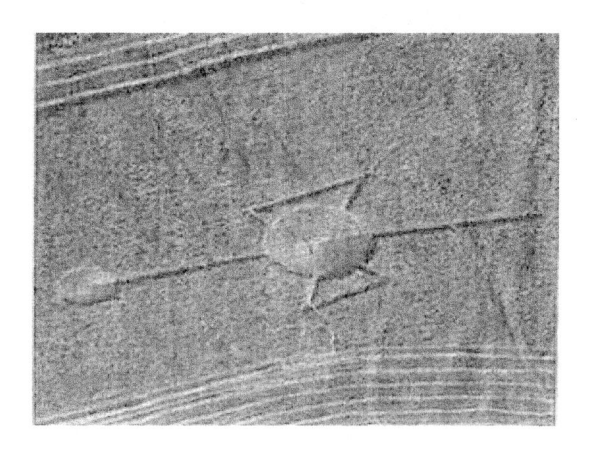

College Ward, Cache Valley, Cache County, Utah – July 20, 1998

Interesting counter-clockwise formation with circles mixed with large areas of randomly downed wheat. Various electro-magnetic effects reported. Circles were of 95, 46, 30, and 30 feet in diameter; the ring was 102 feet. The formation also had connecting pathways between the circles. The entire formation was approximately 316 feet long.

Crop Type: Barley
Source: Jeffery Wilson

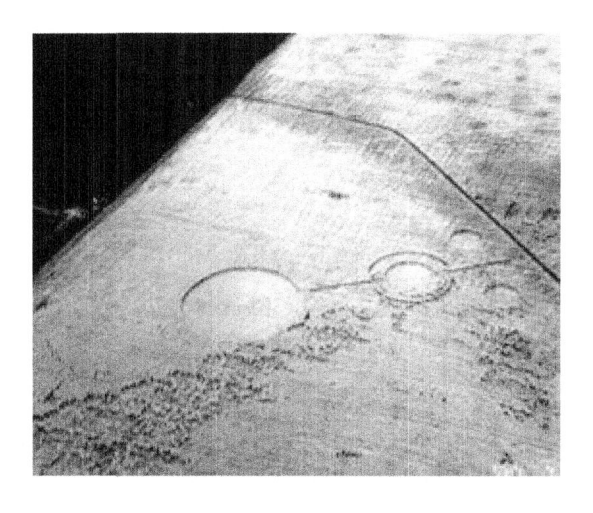

Ryan Skinner and Cheryl Carter

Chapter 14

Cattle Mutilations

Natural, Cults, or Extra-Terrestrial

Over the past thirty years, more than 10,000 animals across the United States have been mysterious mutilated. Mutilation is described as the killing of an animal under unnatural, bloodless, and anomalous circumstances. Although the exact cause has yet to be determined, theories range from natural decomposition, predation, cults, secret government projects, and a popular theory of mere conjecture leads many to believe its extra-terrestrials.

Commonalities among many mutilations are: Farmers report seeing strange balls of light in the sky over the fields prior to discovering the mutilations. Often times animals are heard screaming perhaps due to a sound beyond human hearing range. Dogs appear to be terrified at unseen things. Occasionally, black helicopters are seen in the vicinity at the same time.

The first actually reported strange death of livestock occurred on September 7, 1967, in Alamosa, Colorado. One morning Agnes King and her son discovered one of their cattle named Lady, had met with an untimely death. Upon closer inspection, they found:

- The head and neck had been skinned and defleshed.
- The bones were white and clean.
- There was no blood.
- Strong medical odor.
- A lump of flesh oozed a greenish fluid that burned her hand.
- There were 15 tapering, circular exhaust marks punched into the ground over an area of approximately 5,000 square yards.

She contacted the U.S. Forest Service and Ranger Duane Martin came out. He scanned the area with a Geiger counter which indicated a considerable increase in radioactivity. At first he thought it might be predators, however no explanation as to what caused the mutilation was ever determined.

Strange mutilations began to occur in other places and by 1970 mutilated cattle were reported in 15 states. In May 1979, the Law Enforcement Assistance Administration funded a $44,170 grant that was passed on to the FBI under Title 18 in order to launch a full investigation on the mutilations. It was headed by FBI Agent Kenneth Rommel with the final report released in June 1980 consisting of 297 pages.

The objectives of the investigation were:

- To determine the reliability of the information on which the grant was based, which entailed gathering as much information about the cases as possible about the cases reported in New Mexico prior to May 1979.
- To determine the cause of as many mutilations as possible.
- To determine if livestock mutilations constitute a major law enforcement problem.
- If these mutilations do constitute a major law enforcement problem, to determine the scope of the problem and to offer recommendations on how to deal with it.
- If it is shown that the mutilation phenomenon is not a law enforcement problem, to recommend that no further law enforcement investigations be funded.

Unfortunately, the report concluded that the mutilations were predominately the result of predators and scavenger activity. It also stated that some cases did contain anomalies that could not be identified. However, there have been numerous criticisms of this report. The main reason for this was the lack of forensic and veterinary pathology expertise on the part of Rommel. Moreover, before being appointed as the Lead in Operation Animal Mutilation, his prior expertise had been the investigation of bank robberies.

In 1979, Rommel investigated about twenty mutilations in New Mexico over a six month period. Taking into consideration that he only used a few isolated cases of false positives that were gathered within this extremely short time period to generalize that all animal mutilations were the result of predator/scavenger activity, questions the credibility of the operation as a serious scientific study. Unfortunately, the Rommel Report has been widely cited by some law enforcement agencies and university laboratories to justify not expending resources on further investigations concerning animal mutilation cases.

Ryan Skinner and Cheryl Carter

Cattle Mutilations
NIDS - National Institute for Discovery Science

The National Institute for Discovery Science (NIDS) assumed a different scientific approach to investigating animal mutilations. Unlike Rommel, they conducted field investigations that included necropsies and actual tissue samples. This thirty-three page study included numerous states including Utah. This report reveals twenty mutilations that occurred between 1985-2000 in an area between Vernal nad Roosevelt. www.nidsci.org/articles/animall.html

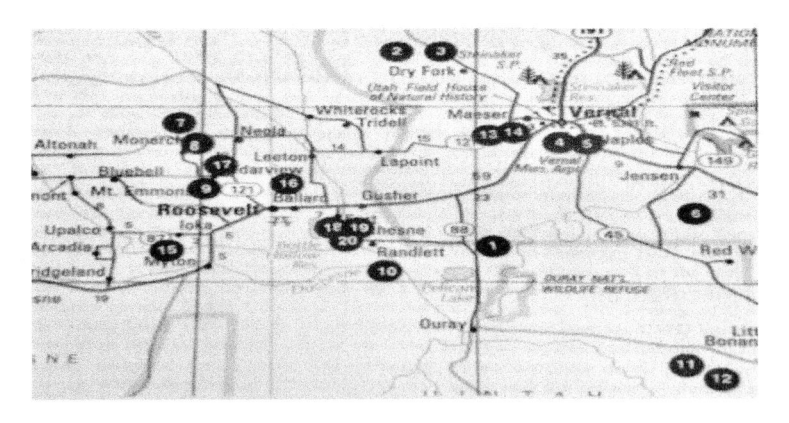

Twenty locations of Animal Mutilation in NE Utah.

Digging Into Skinwalker Ranch

Utah Rancher Case #1

Upon learning of cattle mutilations in the Uintah Basin, The National Institute for Discovery Science (NIDS) conducted a full investigation. The initial reporting is as follows:

March 10, 1996, at 10:00 a.m. two ranchers, Terry and Gwen Sherman, on a remote pasture in NE Utah began the daily tagging of calves born the night before. The weather was bright and sunny with temperatures in the 50s. The ranchers estimated they tagged and weighed the 87 pound animal about 100 yards from the fence line. There was a ring of snow surrounding the pasture where they tagged the animal.

After tagging the animal, they walked about 300 yards west to another newborn animal and went through the process of weighing and tagging that animal. The two were accompanied by their blue heeler dog. About 10:45 a.m. the heeler begins to growl and act strangely with a focus on the area they had just left.

March 10, at 10:454 a.m. the blue heeler begins to snarling in earnest and arching his back. Without warning, the animal ran west across the fields, away from the direction he had been looking. The heeler was never seen again.

March 10, at 10:50 a.m. the rancher and his wife, looking back, then noticed a grown cow running frantically back and forth towards the fence line while dragging her leg. Both then walked back to investigate. The rancher reported seeing the recently tagged newborn calf lying eviscerated in the field (skinned and internal organs removed) close to where it had been tagged about 45 minutes previously. In a 45 minute period in daylight, 100 yards away from any cover, with the rancher about 300 yards away, the calf had most of its body weight removed including entrails, and appeared to have been placed carefully on the ground with no blood present on or near the animal.

March 10 at 4:00 p.m in one of the most rapid times in NIDS investigative history, two NIDS scientific investigators and a veterinarian were standing over the dead calf only a few hours after receiving the call from the rancher. (Figure 1)

(Fig. 1) Animal was found spread-eagled on the grass with blood on or underneath.

The investigators confirmed the eviscerated calf as reported by the rancher. As the veterinarian performed the necropsy, he said a sharp instrument, possibly a knife, had been used to remove the ear. He also reported there may have been evidence of chewing on the animal. The initial observation made by the veterinarian regarding the use of a sharp instrument on the animal's ear was confirmed by an independent veterinary pathology lab. (Figure 2)

(Fig. 2) The animal's left ear had been cleanly cut with a sharp instrument.

A close up of the ear shows the cartilage, hide and all connective tissue had been cleanly sliced to remove the ear. A detached femur bone from the animal was sent to one of the top forensic pathologists in the country who confirmed that two separate sharp instruments had been used on the bone; a heavy machete-like instrument and a smaller scissors-like instrument (Figure 3).

Digging Into Skinwalker Ranch

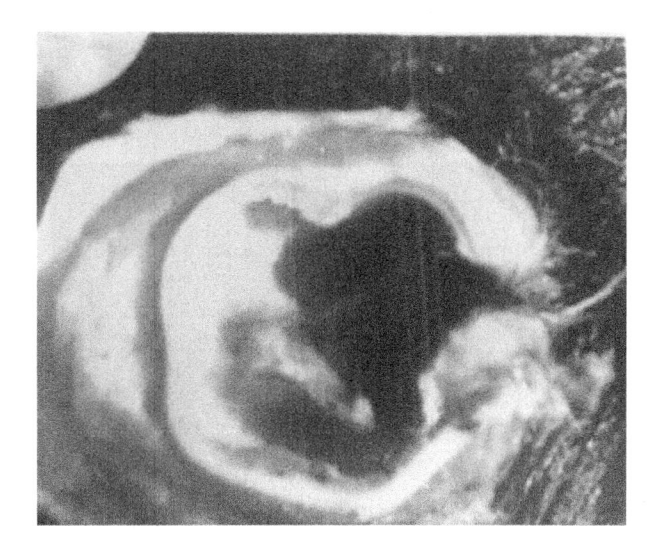

(Fig. 3) Close-up of ear

Within 24 hours, an experienced tracker who makes a living tracking game animals arrived and quartered an area nearly a mile radius from the dead calf. No tracks were found.

No blood was found on or near the animal. The veterinarian who conducted the necropsy had the opinion the animal had been exsanguinated (drained of blood) very effectively. In order to test the hypothesis that blood may have seeped from the animal into the soil. NIDS obtained about three liters of fresh blood (the approximate blood volume of the exsanguinsted animal, using the standard assumption that blood is approximately 7% of body weight) from the local slaughterhouse. The blood was poured on the ground where the calf was found. Videotapes and photographs were recorded of the blood on the ground at regular intervals for 48 hours following the initiation of the experiment. Even 48 hours after the blood was poured, the bright red stain of hemoglobin was very obvious on the grass.

Case #2

At 1600 hours on the afternoon of October 16, 1998, the owner called NIDS to report that his best cow was dead on his property, possibly mutilated. The owner had seen the animal, an expensive registered polled Hereford, in perfect health the previous day. The animal was lying in a waterlogged area of his pasture about 20 feet from a paved road that is used by many local residents (Figure 4).

Digging Into Skinwalker Ranch

(Fig. 4) Shows the position of the animal was lying in when found by the owner.

To preserve anonymity of the owner, we can say that the property is located in the Uintah Basin, Utah. The neighbors were subsequently interviewed and it was determined that there was nothing unusual noticed in the previous or subsequent days that the dead animal was discovered. Immediately, two NIDS investigators, both experienced ranchers and animal mutilation investigators, were dispatched to the scene.

They arrived as it was beginning to get dark, less than two hours after the initial call. According to the investigators, the animal was lying on it's front (sternal recumbency) with front legs tucked in under and rear legs splayed behind. Within feet of the head and sides of the animal the ground was waterlogged. There were no signs of struggle and no visible tracks. Using a compass, the investigator found that the animal was lying in a north-south axis with it's head pointing north. The animal's left ear had been cut off and it's left eye was missing together with a half-inch diameter piece of tissue around the top of the eye. The cut around the eye from visual inspection of photographs appeared to have been made with a sharp instrument (Figure 5).

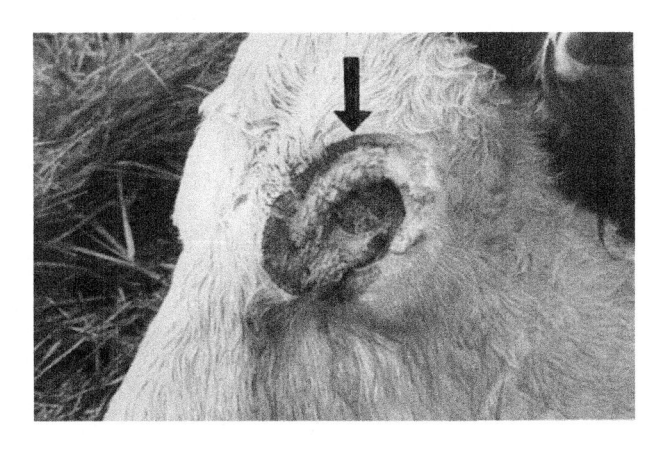

(Fig. 5) Sharp looking cut around the eye.

Both investigators and the owner also noticed an unusual bluish colored gel substance around the eye of the animal as well as on it's anus/vagina and small amount on it's ear. The investigator sampled some of the bluish gel from the anus arae into a test tube and within an hour placed the tube in the freezer (-10° C). He also took a sample of the bluish gel from the eye together with a tissue sample. Finally, he removed a part of the ear that contained the cuts for subsequent historical analysis. A local veterinarian was immediately contacted to conduct a full necropsy. NIDS was informed that because of the lateness of the hour the necropsy would be conducted the next day.

The following morning, October 17, the veterinarian arrived under contract to NIDS to conduct the necropsy. He found:

- The animal appeared to have died instantly on the spot, since there were no signs of struggle.
- Cardiac tissue that was almost unrecognizable. The pericardium (the membrane enclosing the heart) was intact. Investigator described the heart as "shredded." There was no blood in the pericardial sac.
- Enlarged uterus which on palpation yielded no fetus.
- Hemorrhaging around the neck area.
- Cut around the eye: There was a half-inch diameter cut from around the upper eye. Photographic evidence, showing hair that was obviously cut,

suggested strongly that the cut was made with a sharp instrument.

This was confirmed by a veterinary pathologist from Purdue State University and by the NIDS staff veterinarian using a WEsco dissecting microscope equipped with an Olympus digital camera. The photograph (Figure 6) indicates that under low microscopic power, the hair around the eye appeared to have been cut, rather than torn by a scavenger's teeth. It was further established historically that there was NO high heat or cautery used in making the cuts according to veterinary pathologists from Purdue State University and Colorado State University. These two opinions were confirmed by the NIDS staff veterinarian. In summary it was established by three independent experts that the cuts were made with a sharp instrument and not by a predator/scavanger and that no high heat was used to make the cuts. Thus the conclusion is that this appears to be the case in at least a subset of cattle mutilations.

(Fig. 6) Microscopic image of the hair around the eye (x 6.5).

Case #3

In North Carolina, December 29, 2001, the animal; was a seven month premature Charolais calf found with the head skinned and severed at the neck (Figure 7).

(Fig. 7) The hide from the head had been carefully removed before the head was severed.

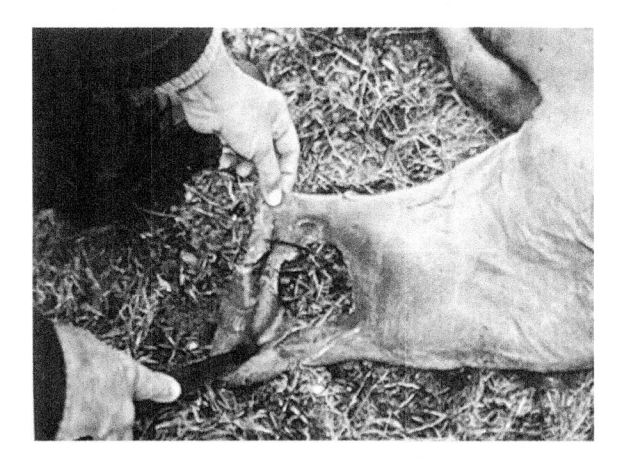

According to the investigator who took the photos, other features included:

- The skull and part of the neck, including muscle tissue were removed.

- The left ear was removed with a semi-circle of flexible hide remaining.
- The right ear was removed with a circle of hide remaining.
- The testicles were cut off in a small round circle. (Figure 8)
- The body was clean, with no signs of afterbirth.
- The body was limber and flexible, with no evidence of rigor mortis.
- The cuts appeared smooth.
- No blood on the hide or on the ground.
- The spinal column had been severed cleanly removing the head.
- The neck under the jaw was cut in a smooth oval.
- The ranchers reported their dogs were barking and upset the night before, a horse came into the yard "for protection," and the family was awakened on the same night by the sound of a helicopter.

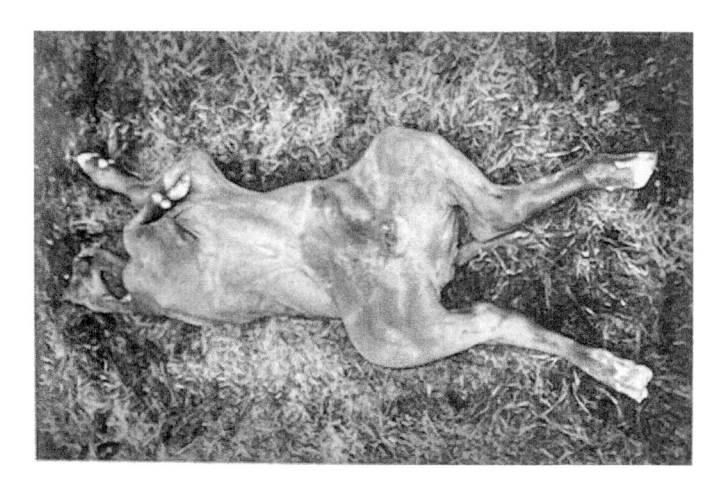

(Fig 8) The animal's testicles had been removed.

These three cases are described as "outliers" and appear to differ from the standard animal mutilation technique. In most of the reports that NIDS has received and investigated, the main focus appears to be on soft tissues, such as lips, tongue, skin and muscles of the lower jaw, rectum and/or genitalia (vulva, vagina, sometimes the entire uiterus, even in pregnancy stage), penis, scrotum (with or without testicles), eyeball (with or without eyelids; usually only one, on the upper side, when the animal is laying on lateral decubitus), tail, mammary gland (the whole udder or teats only), and ears. Due to their nature, location, and accessibility, the removal of these tissues has historically attributed to scavengers or predators.

Digging Into Skinwalker Ranch

A vast body of anecdotal literature exists in the local newspaper archives from 1975-1980 across the nation that documents hundreds, perhaps thousands of animal mutilation reports. Few methodical studies have been conducted, but anecdotal evidence suggests that the eye, ear, tongue, lips, reproductive organs, and anus are most commonly reported missing in these animals. In order to obtain data on animal mutilations, NIDS conducted a survey among 3849 veterinarian bovine practitioners in the United States. Out of the 189 returned questionnaires (Figure 7), 92 reported cattle mutilations and practitioners who replied to the survey reported 39 cases in which the tongue had been removed, 54 cases of documented the removal of an eye, and 70 each for the removal of reproductive organs and rectum (Figure 7).

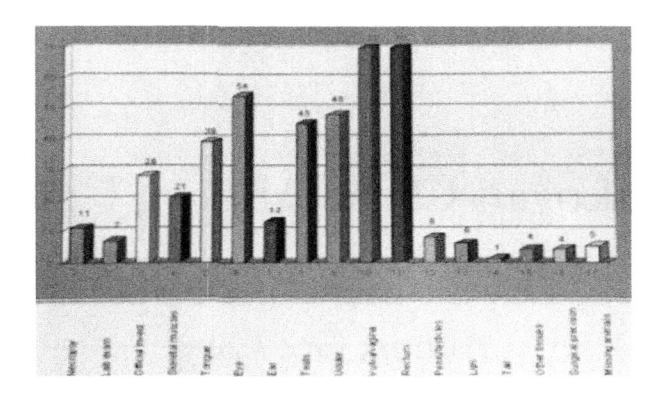

Bovine Practitioner Survey conducted by NIDS indicating the frequency of organs found during animal mutilations.

Ryan Skinner and Cheryl Carter

Vernal Express July 5, 1996
Terry & Gwen Sherman's story of the high strangeness of Skinwalker Ranch including the cattle mutilations.

Verrnal Express Oct 2, 1975
Cattle mutilations in the Willow Creek area and the Cattleman's Association in Salt Lake report.

Logan-Cache Airport, Utah

The Day the Mutilation Perpetrators Almost Got Caught

News of cattle mutilations across the country was common place during the late 1970's and early 1980's. Farmers had so many questions about discovering their cattle either dead or severely mutilated with no explanation. They had their theories that ranged from alien abductions to the United States government conducting tests to determine the levels of radiation in animals.

In 1976, Cache County Sheriff Darius Carter and deputies began to take a stand in order to find some answers. For a time, they had the support of the Utah State Veterinarian in their quest to prove these mutilations were the handiwork of humans. Sheriff Carter believed the government was testing radiation levels in animals. However, at some point, that support was lost.

At first, they were emphatic that there were slices done on the mutilations. Then all of a sudden, they changed their story saying that the cows were being killed by predators such as coyotes. However, Sheriff Carter and his men weren't going to accept that explanation.

The men contended that coyotes rip. You could see on the sides of the animals there were slices made by a knife. Moreover, Sheriff Carter remembered from his earlier days as an X-ray technician that radiation accumulates in the eyes and sex organs of animals. In most of the cattle mutilation cases the animals were missing their eyes and sex organs. How could anyone taking the stance that it was the work of a human, suddenly change their mind and now determine it was predators?

Recognizing the commonality in his county that cattle mutilations were preceded by helicopter sightings the night before, Sheriff Carter and deputies decided to stake the Logan-Cache Airport in an attempt to figure out what had been happening every time multiple unmarked helicopters and airplanes entered the valley only to leave reports of mutilations behind.

In 2001, the National Institute for Discovery Science interviewed a former Cache County deputy concerning what happened that night. The deputy said they observed an unmarked airplane had just landed at the airport. A man wearing shiny, tin-foil-like coveralls rushed over to the aircraft and began loading a suitcase into the plane. Immediately after picking up the cargo, the fixed-wing aircraft started moving again preparing to take off. However, the pilot soon discovered the Cache County Sheriff's patrol car driving down the runway in an attempt to prevent the plane from leaving the ground.

The deputy said he confronted another man who had just jumped out of the pilot side of one of the Huey helicopters. The helicopters were black with no identifying markings. The man was wearing fatigues with no insignia of rank or unit. Then two other helicopters in the air began making what was believed to be a gun pass. Somehow the deputy felt that if he attempted to arrest the man, he would have been killed.

He told the man about the mutilations in the county and that he had been spotted there. He informed him that they had riders with high-powered rifles and sooner or later they would get a shot at his helicopter. They would bring him down if this mutilation does not stop.

The man looked at him and smiled. Then he replied, "May I go now?"

With no reason to hold the man, he got back into his helicopter, took off, and headed west. After that encounter, for the next six years, the cattle mutilations stopped. Sheriff Carter still believes that the government was conducting radiation experiences, but he will never know for certain.

Ryan Skinner and Cheryl Carter

Project Grunge Report 13
Lovette - Cunningham Incident

Project Grunge, February 1949 - December 1949, was the precursor of Project Blue Book which operated from 1951-1969. They both were created to investigate unidentified flying objects. The Air Force's investigation into a reported abduction incident was a 600 page document known as Project Grunge Report 13.

In March 1956, the incident involved two Air Force personnel Sergeant Jonathan P. Lovette and Major William Cunningham of the Holloman Air Force Base in New Mexico. They were searching for scattered debris from a rocket in the White Sands missile testing grounds near the base when Cunningham heard a loud scream. At first he thought Lovette had been bitten by a snake.

However, instead he witnessed him being dragged by a long serpentine arm, wrapped around his legs, and connected to a silver disk that was hovering in the air approximately 15-20 feet away. Cunningham radioed the base for assistance, but by the time they arrived at the location, Lovette had disappeared.

Digging Into Skinwalker Ranch

The base dispatched search parties, but he was nowhere to be found. Base personnel confirmed an unidentified craft on radar at the same time as the incident. Three days later, Lovette's nude corpse was located ten miles from the site of the abduction. The medical examiner stated the body had been severely mutilated. His tongue, eyes, genitalia, and anus appeared to have been surgically removed. The body had been completely drained of blood.

The details of the incident were part of Project Grunge, however this particular report seems to have mysterious vanished.

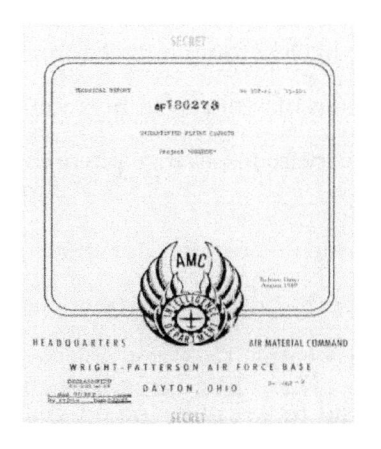

Project Grunge
Wright-Patterson Air Force Base, Dayton, Ohio

Chapter 15

Hitchhikers

There are those you might see standing on the side of the road, thumb in the air, hoping somebody will stop so they might hitch a ride somewhere. Then there are those hitchhikers that you don't see; those lurking within the shadows.

These hitchhikers are entities that attach themselves to living people at a certain location and travel home with them. Why this happens is a mystery. Perhaps it's having the right (or more likely wrong) interaction with a person's energy field. The person may not even be aware of its presence until they begin to experience strange phenomena in their home.

One such location notorious for Hitchhikers is Skinwalker Ranch. Something about these particular entities makes them vengeful. They not only seek out to manipulate you, they intend to wreak havoc on your family members as well. Such is the case with my family.

Ashley VanTassell
Ryan Skinner's Fiancé

"It was February 2019. Ryan was away speaking about Skinwalker Ranch at the Laughlin, NV, UFO Symposium. I had just stepped outside for a few minutes for a quick smoke. When I was finished, I extinguished my cigarette and threw it into the can on the patio.

Upon walking back into the house, the place began to take on an eerie vibe. I couldn't quite explain it, but something was off. Soon I began to hear what sounded like tapping on the walls. Or perhaps, it was just the wind outside. I shook it off as merely my imagination because I was alone in the house.

However, the sounds began to become more frequent, more pronounced and occasionally followed by a bang. Despite my earnest intention to dismiss it, now the cats were acting strange and looking around at things I couldn't see.

Regardless of my adamant conviction that everything was copacetic, there was no denying the doom and gloom feeling I was experiencing. Then after hearing the distinct tapping sound on the wall next to me in the kitchen, I had had enough.

Deciding whatever or whoever was there had commanded enough of my attention, I retired to the bathroom and ran a bath. Afterwards, I was inclined to take some Nyquil in hopes of getting a good night's sleep.

The bedroom is on the main floor close to the stairs. Even though it's a newer house, for some reason the stairs creak. Everyone has their own distinct footstep sound and when I heard what sounded like Ryan running up the stairs it sent chills down my spine. Only minutes before he had texted me saying he was going up on stage soon. Once again I dismissed it as just house noises: just the wind.

Nonetheless, I hurriedly locked the bedroom door and plugged my phone into the outlet next to the bed. For added security, I snuggled with the baby blanket that my aunt had made for me many years ago. It's very sentimental to me especially since she passed in 2007. Soon the Nyquil began to take its affects and I wandered off into dreamland.

Around 3:00 a.m. I was startled awake upon hearing once again what sounded like someone running around the house. My eyes were directed to the fireplace in the wall between the bedroom and living room where there was a strange yellow and orange glow illuminating the room. There was not an actual fire burning in the fireplace so I wasn't sure what was happening.

Now my eyes were diverted toward the door; the door which was now unlocked and slightly ajar. Taking this as sign that I should leave, I reached for my phone, but it wasn't on the night stand. Now I was certain that I had plugged it in, but upon looking around, it was nowhere to be found. I reached for the baby blanket and it too had disappeared. I took that as another sign telling me to leave.

Upon opening the door wider, I realized the strange glow was in all actuality a fire! Once outside, I watched in horror as the back porch was going up in flames. Quickly, I ran bare foot to the neighbor's house and began knocking on their door. They called the fire department which arrived shortly afterward. The firefighter said five minutes more and the entire house would have been engulfed in flames.

After the fire was finally extinguished, the fireman got his flashlight and escorted me back into the house in search of my phone. It wasn't on the floor or under the bed. Then we saw what appeared to be the cable behind the headboard. Pulling the headboard back, there indeed was my phone and charger wedged between the solid wood headboard and wall.

The only way it could have been placed there was for somebody to physically move that heavy headboard.

As he continued to direct his light around the room, there on the floor was the baby blanket perfectly folded as if somebody had placed it there. Had my aunt put it there? Was she the one who woke me up? Was it her who unlocked the bedroom door so that I would be able to make my escape to safety? And who or what had she been protecting me from that night?

The Fire Chief concluded the fire was the result of the burnt support beam holding the porch up. It was the middle of winter, there was no rain or lightning, and yet the beam had the resemblance of a lightning strike. We knew what this looked like because the tree in the backyard had been struck four times on separate occasions. So was it really lightning? It was all just too disturbing that unbeknownst to Ryan, the fire started at the exact same time that he was soon to be on stage speaking about Skinwalker Ranch."

Melissa Peterson
Tyson Skinner's Girlfriend
(Author's Brother)

"It was the summer of 2012. Tyson and Ryan had just returned home from another trip to Skinwalker Ranch. Even though I had never actually been there, it appeared that something had followed Tyson home this time and it decided to come home with me too.

I came down to his place for the weekend wishing the dream would never end. However, upon returning home, my dream had turned into a nightmare.

Exhausted from the trip, I decided to go to bed. Somewhere around 3:00 a.m. I awoke from a sound sleep thinking I had just heard the sound of my doorknob turning. Of course, this had to be a dream, right? Upon opening my eyes something told me to look down the hallway. From my bedroom I have a straight line of sight to my front door.

Suddenly, my eyes fixated on the front door where ... oh no ... the dead bolt was slowly sliding back and forth! It scared me so much that I automatically closed my eyes for a minute. Again, I thought this was surely a dream. Or at least I hoped.

However upon opening my eyes, I saw a large black shadow looming over my entire bedroom door frame. Being paralyzed with fear, I could do nothing but watch as it began to come closer … closer … as if it were reaching for me! I wanted to scream, but instinctively closed my eyes instead.

Before I knew it my nightmare had begun. I felt a warm breath on my forehead that sent chills throughout my body followed by the sensation of something pushing my chest down onto the bed. I couldn't move as it had complete control over me, all the time wondering, "why me?"

Somehow there was a time loss and I woke up again. The bedcovers were disheveled and I found myself at the edge of the bed turned completely sideways. The mere thought of what had happened and else may have transpired that I couldn't remember had me petrified. The following nights my lights were constantly flickering. There was no sign of the shadow man, but I could still feel his foreboding presence.

Not knowing what else to do, I sought the help of a Medium. She said a demon had attached itself to me because I was vulnerable and perhaps going through some personal turmoil at the moment. She advised me to sage my apartment while saying a little prayer. I followed her advice saging for weeks and praying to God for whatever it was to go away … and finally it was gone!"

Whitney Skinner
Ryan Skinner's Daughter

"It was the middle of the afternoon, my father and Ashley who had both just returned from Skinwalker Ranch, had just left to attend a wedding. I was sitting on the couch in the living room looking at my phone. All of a sudden, something in the mirror on the wall caught my attention. At first I thought it was just my eyes playing tricks on me or perhaps it was my over active imagination and the fact that I was all alone. But no, it was real … a big black mass about seven feet tall was floating in front of me!

My heart began pounding and I was really scared not knowing what it was. I watched as it slowly drifted toward the kitchen and behind the partition. Then it came back from the kitchen and floated towards the door.

Now I could sort of make out something that looked like a head, but the rest of it was still a big black mass. Then it got even crazier. When this "thing" got to the door, I actually saw the doorknob slowly turning … turning until the door opened and the black mass drifted outside!

I was SO scared especially since I was alone! I immediately called my Dad to tell him what happened. I know he goes on adventures all the time and sometimes he brings things home with him."

Ryan Skinner's Story

After my rather unsettling encounter with the wolf, I returned to the safety of my home; a place where I can always be assured of finding comfort and solitude. Here, the only thoughts of the wolf would be fleeting flashes in my mind; a mind that would never be quite the same now. In fact, it seemed as though any time I dared to remember that night, even for a few seconds, the wolf knew … it just knew!

One night my dreams were interrupted when suddenly I was jolted from a deep sleep by the distinct sound of three loud bangs on my front door. I instinctively opened one eye as if that would fine tune my auditory perception. Then I fumbled for the clock to check the time … 3:00 a.m. the Witching Hour …supposedly the time when the veil between the living and the dead is the thinnest allowing spirits to travel between two worlds.

For a moment, I laid there staring at the ceiling, or at least where the ceiling would be if it wasn't so dark. *Get a grip, Ryan!* I told myself. Part of me wanted to tune out the sound, but part of me wanted to know who had the audacity to be banging on my door at this time of night.

I jumped out of bed and headed toward the door ready to give this nocturnal intruder a piece of my mind because they obviously needed it. The conversation wasn't going to pleasant for sure.

I reached for the door knob and flung the door open. Taking an authoritative stance, I poked my head out in such a manner as to let this person know I wasn't the least bit impressed that they were calling at this time. However, the only face I saw was that of the moon that looked at me saying, "I got nothing."

"What the hell?" I muttered under my breath. Suddenly, a cool breeze touched my arm and for a moment it felt like finger tips. A chill ran down my spine and I shivered.

Then I remembered that three knocks were supposedly the sign of a malevolent entity. Quickly, I shut the door and reached for the deadbolt compulsively turning it several times as if with each turn it would fortify the lock. Doing my best to shake off that notion, I turned and headed back to bed while being cautious not to catch any reflections in the framed photos on the wall.

The reflections are all in your mind, Ryan! I told myself. I pulled the covers over my head pretending the light on the night stand was a guardian angel. My ears listened intently hoping the silence wouldn't be broken with more knocks.

Had something followed me home from Skinwalker Ranch? I held the covers tighter as if they would shield me from danger. What have I done? I had gone searching for the Skinwalker hoping to tap into its infinite mysteries; seeking to make that special connection so that I might be privy to its power.

However, somewhere along the way, something went array. The Skinwalker was now aware of my intentions … VERY aware. Perhaps it became quite disenchanted with my boldness to become one with it. Now it has decided to teach me a hard lesson. Beware of what you wish. You just might get it!

Suddenly, a not so distant memory flashed through my mind. One night, a fellow investigator and I were near a place known as Werewolf Ridge. We saw three bright lights almost the size of basketballs, yellow, blue, and white, doing amazing things and then dart up the side of the cliff. From there they transformed into a swirling black mass of amorphous matter.

My eyes were unwilling to look at what I might see, and yet, something commanded me to comply. Swirling,

swirling, and hypnotizing me until it morphed into a WOLF! It walked within five feet of me and held me in a penetrating stare for a good five minutes as if it were hungry for my very soul.

For whatever reason, I felt the wolf was what "it" wanted or needed me to see. I think it knew I couldn't handle more than something I recognized. Then the wolf vanished within another swirling black mist and a porcupine appeared. Had this been yet another apparition attempting to gain our trust?

I had attempted to push the incident deep inside my psyche; to compartmentalize it until such time it would be of use. Perhaps tonight the wolf was telling me it was time to revisit the encounter … to say, "What have we learned here?"

Everything was quite now. Whatever I had heard outside has obviously decided to go away. Out of sight, out of mind, right? And yet, I couldn't shake that weird feeling I got as that breeze touched my arm.

Finally convinced that exhaustion was playing havoc on my mind, I decided to try and catch up on my sleep … or so I thought.

For three more nights, this uninvited visitor insistently found great pleasure in waking me up at 3:00 a.m. with its signature three knocks. Each time I opened the door to find a void of emptiness knowing very well this trickster was hiding within the shadows enjoying the hilarity at my expense.

Frustration began to set in as I was beginning to feel like the butt of someone's joke. My irritation heightened more and more each time I turned around and headed back to bed. The words from that poem ran through my mind, "Deep into the darkness peering, long I stood there wondering, fearing" …and I wondered if the next time upon opening the door I would hear a voice whisper, "Nevermore." Oh, if only that were true.

On the fourth night, I was awakened by the sound of the doorbell. Surely there was really somebody there this time. Or had "it" apparently realized it was not achieving the desired effect and decided to employ new tactics?

As I walked towards the door I kept thinking this had better be important. But as usual I was greeted with more nothingness … more nonsense … more messing with my head. At this point I might have called out a few expletives that echoed in the night air.

My sleep pattern began to get erratic. My dreams, more like nightmares, were abundant with shape-shifting monsters lurking within the shadows; their glowing eyes watching … waiting in dire anticipation.

Like I said before, the wolf knows what I'm thinking. It was quite evident when the following night I was not awakened by inquiries and empty salutations. Instead, I was startled to hear the sound of heavy footsteps lumbering toward my bedroom door.

Finally, I came to a consensus that I was no longer going to allow "it" to rent space in my head. I realized that the more I fed into the lucidity of what was happening to me, the more I was unwittingly breathing life into this entity. The more attention I gave it, the more it came alive.

This mysterious entity had acquired a taste for emotions, an appetite for belief and attention, and an insatiable craving to cross over into this world … my world! It had become a living construct of my imagination and it was I who was giving it strength. The demon grew stronger feeding off my self-inflected anxiety. And as it stomped toward my bedroom door, it brought with it the initial stages of possession.

Suddenly a wave of calmness surrounded me as if there was another presence here. With it came a feeling of comfort and protection. Whoever was here instilled in me a knowing of what I should do and how to proceed. Yes, it was all so clear now. *Ryan, you've always had the power. You just had to learn it for yourself.*

On the other side of my door, the mysterious trespasser was growing impatient anticipating my reaction. It began shifting its weight from one foot to the other with each sway causing the wooden floor boards to groan in agony from the sudden weight and then sigh with a creaking relief upon release. Then just for an added effect, it rattled the doorknob. Just for a second, I imagined the door opening finally revealing the identity of my astral intruder.

However, I remained steadfast in my convictions that I was not allowing it any more control over me. I was taking back my power. I was the one in charge now. And just like that, the noise fell silent as my trespasser opted to retreat for the night.

It would be back again and again in hopes of regaining some semblance of power over me. However, it finally realized I was the one in control and retreated back into the ethers.

Despite my better judgment I continued to literally play with fire because after all, there was a fire inside me that could never be extinguished. Never once did I ever consider the ramifications of my sometimes impulsive actions.

Chapter 16
Remote-Viewing The Ranch

Confidential – Final Report

INVESTIGATIVE REPORT:
SHERMAN RANCH ACTIVITIES

PREPARED FOR XXXXXXXXX

JANUARY 10, 2003

Angela Thompson Smith, Ph.D.: Case Manager.

THE NEVADA REMOTE VIEWING GROUP

Ryan Skinner and Cheryl Carter

INTRODUCTION

The following project was presented to The Nevada Remote Viewing Group in October, 2002 and a request made for assistance. Help was requested in identifying the nature of activities at a location in eastern Utah, known as the Sherman Ranch, around 1995 and 1996.

The Nevada Remote Viewing Group is an organization of trained remote viewers who are located around the USA who accept humanitarian remote viewing projects. They also carry out paid remote viewing projects for private individuals, groups, and organizations.

VIEWERS

Two viewers, identified by pseudonyms, initially responded to the project. Later, three additional viewers provided data. The five viewers were tasked with a coordinate, that is, a random series of letters and numbers identifying the project, in this case SR110202. Viewers used a combination of remote viewing methods: Controlled Remote Viewing (CRV) and Extended Remote Viewing (ERV).

The viewers were given operational and directional front loading: *Describe the location and events at this location as of July, 1996.* Apart from the coordinate and operational directions, the viewers worked "blind", that is, they did not know the nature of the project nor did they know of the case manager's discussion with the client. Another two viewers contributed data towards current and future perceptions of the ranch. They were tasked with the directions: *The target is a location, describe any current activity at the location,* and *The target is a location, describe activity at the location in five years ... Skinwalker Ranch.*

SUMMARY

The indications, from the first two viewers who completed Phase One, were that this was the site of a military operation, probably conducted by the Navy. There were individuals at the site involved in "target practice" with rifles that involved lying prone on the ground. Men in uniform, such as policemen, firefighters, or soldiers were present. Several oblong devices were described.

A sketch and description of a male and identifying injuries or tattoos were described. There is a project ongoing at the site that involves cartographers and maps of the United States. Most of the activity appears to take place outdoors, at night. The three additional viewers perceived gridded and honeycomb surfaces, a flat surface and one that was rounded like a globe. The interior and functioning of the globe was described. Two viewers felt wave-like, seismic vibrations.

Current activity at the location indicated a series of installations having been built including a grid-work of wires and small platforms that have been embedded in the ground at the location, a tall, TV like antenna, and a communications-type building.

Future activity, five years from now, indicates that a fire, either caused by nature or accidental will have burned the communications-type building and a parcel of land surrounding the tower and building.

THE NATIVE SPIRIT KNOWN ONLY AS "THE TRAVELER"

BY BAASS

Communicates to research via Automatic Writing after experiment session on Ranch

Day 2 of "Skinwalker Ranch" experiment:

"I saw flashes of images in my mind. I heard song and crying. Drums and wailing. I saw fire and fighting. I saw peace and day to day life. I saw man laying dead on the ground."

BREAK

"I saw the spirit of these men fill into the bodies of the animals on the land and ascend into the trees, the plants, the birds. The ground is sacred. A slaughter happened and I felt it. I couldn't see who or what it was that did this but the life of men and animals became the protectors of the mother earth. Protectors from the sky beast."

BREAK

"The Sky beast land. Take our women. Take our children. Kill the man. Kill the chief. Take animals that feed us, animals that protect us. They take them while we fight. We sing our war song and send it into the sky. They are not like us. They are not like animal on land or sky. They fly and have no expression on face. They take one man, but kill us all. We fight, we cry for our chief. We lost a great deal. They do not speak. They are strong. They do not bleed. They are big and stand tall next to me. My brothers and sisters are gone, they take everything and we are gone from this earth. They leave quickly with beasts and our women and children."

BREAK

"One man. Why take them? Why one man? Why kill our tribe? Why did our animals go? Why take man? How not bleed? How not look like man? Tall, long arms, long stick like legs, large head, and hands like man but less. Large head with eyes missing two places where they should be. Mouth doesn't move. Beast from sky move slow and I lay still so they stay away. I lay still so they go. They stay on land. Have something in sky. Big light in the sky. By big light they travel, fire is going out, and all my brothers are gone, dead by me but one in sky, one man with children and women. Chief gone. Chief gone. Chief gone. All is gone. Beasts walk slow and don't talk but leave me as I lay. I lay half in water. I wait for beast to leave. Sky lights go away. And take beasts and women and one man. They leave us here. I wail in the loss. I wail for my tribe and sing to my ancestors. At nightfall I dance by fire. I call beast back. I am ready to fight sky beast as a man wolf. I am ready for them and waited for many moons. I dance and wait and call to my ancestors for sky beasts to bring my family, my children, my tribe. They return after 7 moons in darkness. They come to bring more sky suns…the light bright to deliver men but not who I remember. The men are of my color but not my family. My children they are not. My wife they are not. The beasts return with new men new animals but not my brothers and sisters. Not my tribe. They look like me but their eyes do not see me. They look, but not see. They march. They do not sing for return. They do not dance for return. They walked still. They sit and look up at stars and do not see me. The beasts have brought animals but look like them. They do not make sound, no sound. No sound from men and women or animals."

BREAK

"The sky beasts leave 27 men and 43 women. Children do not return. My heard of horses are few and cows are only 3. They make no sounds. They do not look at me. Sky beast leaves and all sound return. All men and women speak in my tongue and move like they belong. Move and speak like sky beast had not taken them. Who are these men and women? Who are they? They look like me, but different. They still don't see me and do not come towards me. I move careful. I move to talk. I move close but they don't see me. It is night. They build shelter quickly, build with ease and might. Build fire, build surroundings, grow food and have babies. Babies look like me, but have something new. They are like me and like sky beast. They do not cry like my children did."

BREAK

"They are strong and grow fast. I watch for many moons, sky beast return but four times in my years. I am safe. I have learned to be one with them and to keep my body cleansed by the earth. After many more moons I am old man. I am slower than the new tribe. There are many families, many more have grown into what looks like me. I live among them not knowing if any are my children the sky beasts took so long ago. I am old, I am tired. I have learned some of their ways but keep myself with wolves and bear. I watch sky and wait for return. They come, they will take all things you love, all things from man and earth they keep and return new life, the life is not like my people, they live in the light in sky. Sky beast don't create harm to me or others, but fear what man has done. They do not come until they need, but will bring back something, something like you, something like them. Watch the sky. Watch the life around you and be one with mother earth, with her animals and plants and sky, be one so you know the ways of them. When sky beasts come they see but not like us, they give but not like us, they will bring your women and men but not the same. Know your earth creatures and you will know when sky beasts come."

BREAK

"I am man that hides among the sky beast. My spirit stays on this earth to give message of my people to those who seek truth. Those who seek the light from sky beast, be ready for them. If you seek, have your hide so you can see among your people."

Medium, Remote-Viewer, Ojibwe
Remote-View Session, 12 Mar 2021

Remote-viewing is the ability to acquire accurate knowledge about a distant place, person, or event without using any physical senses or equipment. It is also known as "anomalous cognition."

The Beta waves in the temporal cortex, otherwise known as "Broadmann Area 37" of the brain, located behind the right ear, usually measure 38 Hz. When a medium has reached peak concentration, the waves suddenly explode into Gamma waves which can measure as fast as 100 Hz.

Cheryl Carter Remote-View of Skinwalker Ranch
12 March, 2021

"As soon as I began to remote-view at the Ranch, a Native woman approached me. She was young, perhaps twenty, with her hair in one braid. She was holding a small child in her arms … a boy … his eyes closed and body very still. He looked to be about two years old.

She saw me … our eyes met … and she had tears falling from her brown eyes. She was filled with both anger and sadness.

"They killed my baby!" she cried. "The animals killed my baby!" … I saw a herd of sheep nearby, but no fence.

She came closer and said, "Help my baby, Medicine Woman!" … sadly, I could not help her nor get her to understand. She finally sat down on the ground still holding her son in her arms.

Soon I got another vision of her wrapping the child in a blanket along with a small rattle made of a turtle shell with seeds inside … but she couldn't bury him there … the land was "spoiled." … it needed to be sacred ground. So she carried him up to the ridge and buried him there.

Then I saw a very tall Native man. He was about thirty with finely chiseled features with his hair in one braid. On his head, a single feather was attached to a thin rawhide band. He was not wearing a shirt … his body was muscular … a thin strap of leather was tied around his right forearm. He stood on the bank of a stream near a grove of trees …

holding a bow in his hand ... a beaver dam on his left with two beavers ... a Medicine Man.

I felt as though I had seen him before .... that I somehow knew him ...then I realized ... yes, we had met before. This was the same man, "Stands Looking", that has been appearing to me at Lodge for six years! ... 1700 miles away ... He wants me to see something there, but does not speak of what that is.

Soon I got another vision of him gathering small pieces of wood ... he was a "Firekeeper" building a sacred fire for ceremony. He also collected many medium size rocks that would be called "Grandfathers" and put them into the fire. These are used for Lodge sometimes referred to as Sweat Lodge.

After lighting the fire, he began the ritual of connecting the physical world to the spiritual world. He put some tobacco ... we call it "asemaaa" ... into his pipe. (Tobacco is used to connect two worlds because the roots of the plant grow deep into the Earth and its smoke rises high up into the heavens. The fire in the pipe represents the fire in the sun; the smoke symbolizes the truth being spoken.)

He takes a puff of the pipe and raises it to the sky as he calls out to the Four Directions ... (i.e. I call to the West with its life giving rains and spirit world, to the North with strength and honesty, to the East where the sun rises and brings us knowledge, and to the South that brings us bounty, medicine, and growth.)

Then with a shovel, he carefully removed seven rocks from the fire placing them into a pit located inside the Lodge. He crawled inside and threw some water onto the hot rocks causing a steam to fill the area ... he sat awaiting visions ... the spirit of a wolf came in and sat at his left side.

He puts something into an underground cave ... items that are of great importance to him.

This man who died at a young age, the result of a hunting accident, is a constant protector of the land ... has been here a very long time ... watching for the Sky People ... watching the flickering lights of the Elementals ... beings belonging to the Earth that are neither human nor animal.

A ball of orange light ... intelligent ... knowing. A portal opens ... rumbling beneath the ground ... passageways that extend for a long distance.

I was being drawn to the far side of the property ... Russian Olive trees ... voices whispering ... can't hear what they are saying or perhaps they don't want me to hear ... an abundance of Elementals present ... shadow people.

Another vision of a time much nearer, this time of a Homestead ... a woman is cooking dinner inside ... I can smell the beans ... laughter of children outside ... two young children, a boy and girl, chasing each other ... unbeknownst to the family, they are living among other-worldly beings ... some good ... some not so much ... watching unsuspected."

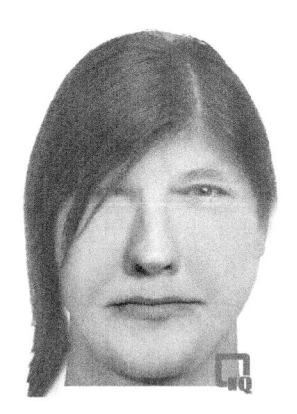

© Cheryl Carter
Drawn with my Composite Software

Chapter 17

Implants

One day after returning home from a recent adventure, I noticed a small lump on my forearm. Upon touching it, I was concerned to find what appeared to be something moving inside. My first thought was that it was most likely a cyst and would probably go away in time.

During the following weeks after my discovery, I began to hear disembodied voices. It sounded as if two people were having a conversation. It wasn't clear what they were saying because it was almost like white noise. Instantly, my mind went to the science fiction notion that perhaps I was the owner of an implant.

When I realized the lump wasn't going away, I contacted Doctor Doug Hobson to have whatever it was examined and hopefully removed. He confirmed that it wasn't a cyst, but there was actually something interesting under the skin. I asked him the doctor to remove it and he obliged. Once excised, he found it was almond-shaped and appeared to contain quartz and silver. The origin was undetermined.

Now concerned that it might be some sort of implant, I contacted Wisconsin MUFON for some additional testing.

Here I was in communication with several field investigators including Chuck Modlin, Tim White Eagle, David Watson, and Vicki LeBlanc.

They requested that I send them the sample for further examination. They also suggested that I have a CPK test to find if my body had elevated levels. They said for reasons unknown to them, it appears this test may be elevated if someone has had an abduction experience. When my doctor tested me, he did in fact determine I had elevated levels of CPK.

I released my specimen and doctor's records to MUFON for further investigation. Upon analyzing my specimen under an electron microscope, it was determined its components contained silver and quartz wrapped in neural fibers. These materials are often used in building transistors and not anything that would normally be found in the human body.

In the end, the results of my specimen were still inconclusive and furthermore, I was not able to move any further on this for the fact that my specimen was never returned to me and was somehow determined "lost." One thing I do know for sure is that immediately after the removal

Digging Into Skinwalker Ranch

of the implant the majority of the dramatic and strange encounters both on and off the Ranch immediately stopped.

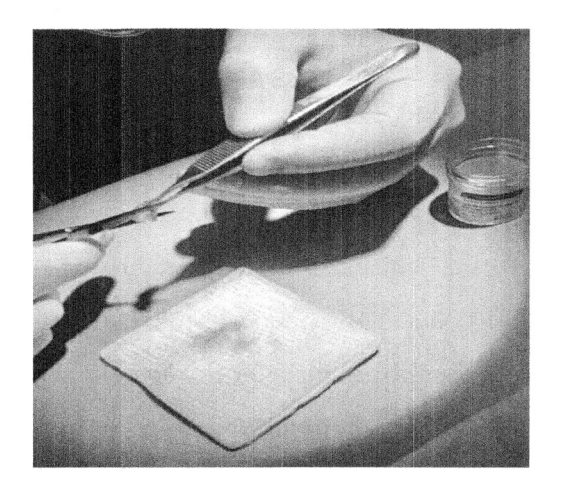

Sample taken from my arm

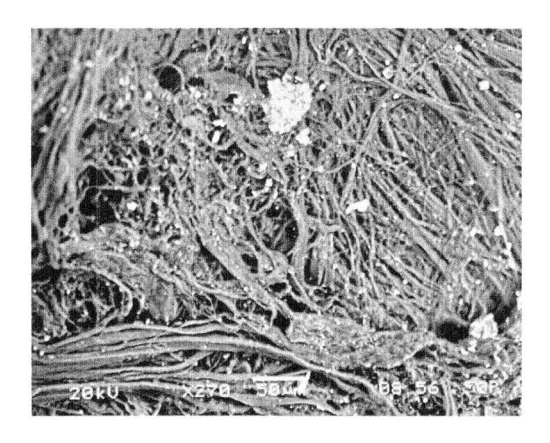

Close-up electron microscope view of the implant that the doctor said had neural fibers wrapped around it.

Coincidentally, Christopher Bartel a former Guard at the Ranch discovered two small lumps as well:

"One night while on patrol, we encountered a wolf, but it was twice the size of an ordinary wolf. Then a short time later I noticed two strange lumps that felt like there was something inside; one on my knee and the other on my right forearm. I finally went to the VA and the doctor examined them. He also did an MRI, but it was inconclusive. He thought they were just cysts. I still have them to this day, but they don't bother me." When asked if the object inside him was an implant Chris replied, "It is the Ranch so anything is possible."

Chapter 18
No Trespassing

As we headed down the path, the evening sun began to cast shadows on the ground. Knowing where we were at the moment, somewhere near Werewolf Ridge, shadows could represent almost anything. With that thought in mind, we were in a constant state of intense observation just in case.

By the time we finally reached Werewolf Ridge, the sun had already escaped from our view. Now the big orb in the night sky was the only light to guide us. The three of us paused for a few minutes to catch our breath. This was the first adventure for my friend Brian who was a total skeptic. Sometimes it's interesting to have a skeptic's point of view. Everything that goes bump in the night isn't always of any concern and many times can be explained. Or at least, that's what we thought.

It was totally dark now and we began to notice little flickers of blue lights dancing around us.

"It's just fireflies," Brain remarked.

I had seen fireflies before, but they are always yellow. These were blue. I couldn't discern any actual substance to them, but the blue lights continued to flicker. Whatever it was, it appeared to be intelligent. Suddenly, they floated closer to Brian in a playful manner. And just like that, he stopped in mid sentence and nodded off to sleep. How weird was that?

We are SO close to gaining access to the Ranch, our adrenaline on high, and he just falls asleep. Was he that worn out from our two hour trek? Or had the flickering blue lights had an effect on him?

My other friend and I sat there a few minutes deciding what course of action we would pursue. Occasionally, our conversation would be interrupted by a snort from our sleeping companion. It was dark that night, very dark. What better opportunity for us to finally take the chance and sneak into the Ranch. It would be my first time trespassing.

Soon the flickering blue lights faded away. Then out of the darkness emerged a porcupine. This was the second time I had witnessed a porcupine on the path. We watched as the animal, completely oblivious to our presence, slowly walked over to where Brain was sleeping. It began to sniff him out as all animals do, his face and his hands. Then when it moved down to the family jewels it gave him a slight nibble.

Even being fast asleep, a man is totally aware of protecting such things. Instinctively, Brian shot up and started jumping around.

"What the f*ck!" he shouted and he started jumping as if his hair was on fire.

With that the porcupine blended into the darkness. When he finally calmed down, he said he was as surprised as we were that he just dozed off because he hadn't felt tired. Perhaps those flickering blue lights wanted to teach the skeptic a lesson.

We told Brian that while he was sleeping we had made some plans contingent of his input. Reaching an immediate consensus, we began our adventure by scaling down the ridge. Our targeted destination was an old shed near Homestead 2 that was just across the creek against the Mesa.

As we drew nearer to the shed, I realized how much danger we could be in at any moment. Should one of the guards observe us trespassing, we would be handcuffed and arrested. However, crazy as it seemed, there was something about the danger that excites me.

What would we find inside the shed? I suspected it would be computer and surveillance equipment. My eyes scanned the area looking for any indication we had been spotted by a guard. Everything looked good. The door was partially opened enticing me to come in. I nervously reached out, my heart beating faster, and as it opened it made a creaking sound.

We entered the shed, but much to our disappointment there was nothing exciting inside. The paint that had once covered the walls had long since begun to chip, peel, and curl. And yet despite their appearance, they continued to maintain their dignity. In the middle of the room, was a lone folding lawn chair perhaps used by a guard during his nightly rotation. I noticed an interesting polished river rock and decided to slip it into my pocket. Perhaps that was a mistake.

After being in the shed only about five minutes, we decided to explore somewhere else hoping to engage in something more exciting because, "This is why we are here!" Beware of what you wish.

Instantly, I noticed to the east an orange ball of light approaching us from across the field. Was it one of the guards? But it couldn't have been because as it got closer we noticed it was too high in the air to be a person.

"Let's get the Hell out of here!" I warned.

Without hesitation, the three of us started toward the trail to the West Gate. We turned one last time to observe the orange light flying in the direction of the shed and hovering over it. It was as though it knew we had trespassed and was making certain we had not disturbed anything. But wait ... I had ... and the river rock was in my pocket was proof.

Then with the knowledge of my indiscretion, the orange light focused on us and a chase ensued. My adrenaline began surging like a runaway train and I instantly turned into survival mode.

"Run!" I yelled as the orange light raced after us in hot pursuit. Brian the skeptic, now a true believer, was leading the way. The darkness began surrounding us, consuming our very thoughts. I feared my heart would beat out of my chest and that's probably exactly what "it" wanted.

"Look!" my other friend shouted as he pointed ahead. There blocking our path to the Gate were not guards, but two shadow people. A quick look over my shoulder and the inevitable was realized. We were going to be dealt with by forces beyond our comprehension. Would they remove us from this place and send us into a portal or another dimension? At this point, all three of us wished we could mend the error of our ways.

Then as if our thoughts became theirs, the two shadow figures parted and blended into the foliage on either side of the road. Quickly, we ran around the Gate hoping to escape. And as we did, the orange light, satisfied with our departure, flew back into the ethers of the Ranch.

I slipped my hand into my pocket feeling the texture of the river rock; my treasure, my trophy. I paused for a moment and looked over my shoulder for one last glimpse. This wasn't good bye of that I was certain because I knew we would be meeting again.

Ryan holding his River Rock.

Chapter 19
Within the Shadows of the Ridge

The desert sun began to relinquish its hold on the day and slowly slip out of view behind the mesa. Like the flame of a candle, it would soon quietly extinguish and fade to black. Ryan Skinner's brother Tyson looked on as his brother headed over the ridge and watched until his shadow receded.

He stood there a moment appreciating the beauty of the landscape. He was glad Ryan persuaded him to accompany him on this adventure. He wasn't a true believer in all the mysteries of this place. However, unbeknownst to him he would soon become one.

He gripped the walkie-talkie in his hand as if it were a live hand grenade of which he had just pulled the pin. He was disappointed that they had traveled for three days only for him to sprain his ankle preventing him from being able to explore. This radio in his hand would be his only means of adventure that night as he had to solely rely on his brother's updates. Little did he realize at the moment the adventure he himself was about to embark on.

He walked back to the tent, but turned one last time looking at the trail. He was grateful to be afforded the opportunity to experience this place. Perhaps after getting some rest he might be able to tap into the many mysteries Ryan had told him about.

The radio chirped as his brother called making sure they were getting a good signal.

"Yep, I can hear you fine," he replied. "Going to bed now."

He pulled down the zipper and crawled inside the tent. Once inside, he attempted to find a comfortable position for his aching ankle and prepared to get some sleep. Well, at least he tried.

"Looks like we're alone now," a disembodied voice whispered in his ear.

Thinking it was just the wind, he wrapped his arms around his head in hopes of muffling the sound. Why does the silence make you hear things that aren't there? Sleep … he just needed some sleep.

Soon he was abruptly awakened by the sound of distant gun shots. With one eye opened, he listened intently …thud … thud … thud. What was that sound? It was so close. Could it be the sound of his panicked heart? No, it was the sound of distant gunshots. What were those gun shots? Did somebody from the Ranch just kill his brother? Suddenly, he heard the sound of an engine idling outside his tent lightly feathering the gas. He felt his heart rise up into his throat. Were they now here to kill him too?

He quickly sat up, tried to catch his breath and focus on his next move. Springing into survival mode, his next thought was to get out of the tent and make his escape. He wasn't sure where he was going, but running like hell sounded like a great idea.

However, before he could carry out his plan, a strange sensation came over him. A malevolent vibe surrounded him with a cloak of darkness and began to consume him. Seconds later, he found himself paralyzed and unable to move. Somebody or something was holding him down and they were in control now. Then he remembered the same voice whispering in his ear that he so easily dismissed.

He wasn't quite certain if he was hallucinating or if it were real, but a myriad of faces began to flash before his eyes;

faces of people he had never seen before. They kept flashing, flashing at an incredible speed; strangers of different ages, men and woman. And yet, his mind was able to comprehend every detail of their faces. Who were these people? Did something bad happen to them here? Is this a warning to anyone who trespasses on this land? Who was holding him captive and projecting these images into his mind?

All he knew was something about them was horrifying, so horrifying that he wanted to scream, but he couldn't. The entire time the radio would screech communications from his brother. "Tyson, can you hear me?" … "Tyson, talk to me!" If only he could manage to get control of his fingers so he might reach the red button, but alas all he could do was wish it away.

After what seemed like forever, what sounded like the sound of the running car stopped. Had they gone away? Moments later, his left pinkie began to twitch a little, then a toe wiggled, and soon he could move his entire body. As soon as he felt strong enough, he hurried out of the tent. He looked around, but there was no sign of a vehicle or any guards. In fact, there were no tire tracks anywhere.

Suddenly, a strange rustling sound coming from the grove of Russian Olive trees about 500 feet away commanded his attention. He thought it was rather odd since there didn't seem to be any breeze. Then he assumed the sound was birds, literally hundreds of birds that appeared to be unusually agitated. And yet, he never saw any.

Soon the mysterious sound that he had heard coming from the direction of the Russian Olive trees became exceedingly intense and he watched as a huge black mass appeared; whirling, ever-changing, in an almost hypnotizing pattern. The mere sight was unnerving. Then he gasped as the formation suddenly morphed into the shape of a creature … a demon-like monstrosity with a huge wing span of about twenty to thirty feet, flapping its wings as it hovered directly over him.

A few seconds later, a bright light flashed on the mesa behind him; a light so large he surmised that it must have been mounted on a jeep. However, that would have been impossible given the craggy terrain which surrounded him. Even a man would have a difficult time scaling the craterous landscape. Then the spotlight shown upon him bathing him in an unholy light as if the demon was announcing its malevolent power. Was this some sort of foreboding message; a warning of things to come? He stood frozen, terrified, and alone in the dark desert with Ryan nowhere to be found.

Quickly, he grabbed the radio realizing how we take for granted the use of our hands. His trembling fingers searched desperately for the talk button.

"Ryan, something is shining a light on me!" the panic very evident in his voice.

"What happened? I've been trying to call you." But the radio only hissed followed by a long silence. "Tyson, talk to me!"

"I can't talk now! It's all over me! Get back here!"

No matter how many times I tried to contact my brother there was not a sound coming through from his end; not a chirp or a screech. Fearing he was in danger, I abandoned my post on Werewolf Ridge and began to run as fast as I could back to the campsite. I didn't dare turn on my light for fear of being spotted by a guard. Instead, I took my chances in the total darkness with only the stars to guide me, sometimes tripping along the way, but onward to my brother.

Upon reaching the campsite, there was no sign of him. Most likely he was inside the tent. Slowly, my hand began to unzip the flap; the mere sound breaking the utter silence that surrounded me. It seemed that whatever was out there had decided to leave us alone. Or did it? Hesitation overtook me as I wondered what I would find inside. A myriad of thoughts raced through my mind. Would I find my brother peacefully sleeping? Would he be crouched in the corner squeezing himself deeper into the darkness hoping whatever was outside wouldn't find him? Or was something holding him captive and waiting insidiously for me to arrive?

"Tyson are you ok?"

He looked at me for a few seconds and replied, "I need a drink. Come join me."

Chapter 20

Beyond the Continuum

The past, present, and future are intrinsically one with the land. It is apparent to those who have been afforded the opportunity to engage with the anomalous phenomena and other-worldly beings traversing the time-space continuum of this place. As a result, they embrace the duality of the uniqueness as well as the mystery. And most importantly, they come to realize an everlasting alliance; a oneness that will forever be held deep within their heart for this place called ...

Skinwalker Ranch

Printed in Great Britain
by Amazon